Traveling Light

A *Lillenas* DRAMA RESOURCE

Traveling Light

*Mark's Complete Gospel in
70 Scenes and Monologues*

by Lawrence G. Enscoe

Lillenas PUBLISHING COMPANY

KANSAS CITY, MO 64141

To my mother

For understanding why I needed
glue at midnight,
for enduring a garage filled with Mount Sinai
and papier-mâché,
for putting up with sore ears from listening
to my ideas,

and for telling a little boy
he could do anything

Contents

Including References in Mark and Character Assignments

A Word About Traveling Light

It isn't every year that a manuscript like *Traveling Light* comes across an editor's desk. When it does, the world lights up and bells ring. At the risk of sounding overly enthusiastic, let me say that Lillenas is extremely proud to be the publisher of this work and believes that churches and theater groups everywhere will stage it to the glory of God.

Larry Enscoe piqued my anticipation with what could be done dramatically with the Gospel of Mark back in 1988, when he presented a selection of monologue-scenes at the annual Lillenas Music and Drama Conference. From that performance I began a continued nudging and cajoling for Larry to expand his much-toured, highly successful one-man presentation.

When our gifted playwright finally began the project, he realized that selectivity was not going to be satisfactory—the script had to encompass the total book. During those writing months, the telephone calls between Pasadena, Calif., and Kansas City were frequent and overflowing with serious discussion about how best to contemporize these familiar characters and events from Mark. The young author found himself taking on the disciplines of a seminary student as well as a dramatist. The fine art of biblical interpretation (hermeneutics) mixed well with theatricality.

The name Lawrence G. Enscoe appears on six books in the Lillenas catalogue—two with his wife Andrea. None is more important than the book you hold in your hand. I believe it will become the source for countless sermon sketches, Easter and Lenten presentations, as well as full-evening performances of Christ's life and ministry in settings that come awfully close to the world in which we live.

As publisher of *Traveling Light,* we at Lillenas send out this drama resource with a prayer for its influence in your ministry.

PAUL M. MILLER
Lillenas Drama Resources

Production Notes

AS MONOLOGUES

Traveling Light was written to be used as a year-round dramatized Scripture resource for sermons, services, programs, classes, and seminars. Nearly all of the 70 scenes that follow can be used as stand-alone monologues or scenes.

The stage directions give you all the information you'll need as to character, costume, props, and sound cues. Look for the first time the character appears in the story for the most information on how to perform him or her.

AS A FULL-LENGTH PLAY

Traveling Light was also created to be done as a single event. Three actors—two men and a woman—enter the stage as FIRST TRAVELER, SECOND TRAVELER, AND THIRD TRAVELER. With those initial characters established, they move on to play the nearly 40 characters who tell the Gospel story.

In a little over 90 minutes, an audience will have seen Mark's Gospel in its entirety—in a way they've never seen it before.

With a little adjustment in the opening scene, you can also add in as many actors as you want to play the characters. There are a maximum of 17 roles for women, 24 roles for men.

COSTUMES

The costumes are all designed to give the audience a quick assessment of the type of character the actor is portraying. The stage directions give some clear options. When making wardrobe choices, make sure the audience can identify the costume and props without hesitation.

If you're doing the full-length version, keep the costumes simple. There isn't much time for changing during the play. Actors can go offstage to change or—as the stage directions indicate—pull the jackets, hats, glasses, etc., from the trunks. They then can put them on in front of the audience. Once a costume is pulled out of the trunks for a character, it can be placed around the stage for easy access. This is especially helpful for recurrent characters like Peter, Thomas, Levi, etc.

MUSIC/SOUND EFFECTS

Because musical bridges and sound effects are so important to the spirit and mood of this play, Lillenas has produced a compact disc (MU-9144T) containing all the music and effects necessary for staging the full script or portions of it. See the inside front cover for details.

The author has planned these musical "breathers" as mood enhancers for moving out of one scene and into the next. They also provide space for costume and prop changes.

If you are performing *Traveling Light* as a full-evening work or scenes in a worship service, you will find the music and sound effects, written and recorded by Craig Paddock, a valuable addition to the performance. The variety of sound effects make this a valuable tool for other productions.

The script provides a reference number for each music and sound effects cue.

Make sure to schedule adequate rehearsal time for your sound tech to get comfortable with the cues (there are a few tight ones that demand special attention) for actors and crew to perform costume and prop changes in the musical time provided, and be aware of the length of scenes where music underscores dialogue. All fade outs will be handled manually by your sound person.

THE SET

The set is meant to be simple and open. Trunks, chairs, a signpost, and standing upstage flats, perhaps, for actors to go off and grab costumes and props. Make use of the space when blocking.

LIGHTING

Lighting can go a long way to set mood and keep the scene changes crisp. If lighting is limited, then use the music and sound effects in place of fade-outs or blackouts, and as time buffers, allowing the actors to put on characters' costume pieces in front of the audience.

PROPS

Props are few. And they should be absolutely necessary to the characters to avoid time lag and actor trip up.

BLOCKING

The director should take his or her cue from Mark, which moves quickly from place to place, person to person. Some emotional scenes might want to have a little longer setup—e.g., when Jairus comes forward and begins his testimony; but for the most part, things should zip along, unfolding a passionate, purposeful, and powerful Gospel before the audience.

Use the whole space—and create levels. Don't allow all actors to deliver their monologues only downstage. Characters might have a favorite place they always go to on the stage, however.

CHARACTER

All the biblical participants have been assigned American types. Make strong character choices so that the spectrum of individuals is clear.

Don't be afraid of accent, idiom, and dialect—Southern, New England, L.A., Midwestern. But make sure they're not too outrageous. The audience has to believe you're who you say you are.

The Characters

FIRST TRAVELER

SECOND TRAVELER

THIRD TRAVELER

(NOTE: If you are performing Traveling Light *as a full-length play, the* THREE TRAVELERS *play all 38 characters below.)*

JOHN THE BAPTIST, a fiery street preacher

BELIEVERS, John's disciples

PETER, a Brooklyn longshoreman

PETER'S MOTHER-IN-LAW, a feisty Jewish woman

THE LEPER, an AIDS patient

THE DOCTOR, the leper's examiner

THE PHOTOGRAPHER, the leper's chronicler

THE PARALYTIC, a Vietnam vet

BUDDY, the paralytic's friend

LEVI, a nerdy, high-strung tax man

THE CONSTRUCTION WORKER, an earthy, blue-collar type

THE BOOMER, a snobby exec

MARY, the heartaching mother of Jesus

JESUS, the passionate, indefatigable Son of God

THE RANCHER, a tough, laconic Texas herder

JAIRUS, a conservative business leader

KING HEROD, a scary mobster type

THE BARBER, Herod's wise-guy attendant

THOMAS, a surfer-dude college student

THE GENTILE WOMAN, a harried diner waitress

THE FATHER, a New England lineman

LITTLE CHILD, a precocious five-year-old

THE LAWYER, a high-powered legal rep

THE MOM, a career-plus-motherhood mom

RICH MAN, a corporate fund-raiser type

BARTIMAEUS, a grungy, disenfranchised blind man

TOURIST ONE, an obnoxious small-town gawker

TOURIST TWO, ditto

CARNY MAN, a creepy con artist

COURT REPORTER, a shy, sincere stenographer

THE WIDOW, a welfare mother

JUDAS, an addict

CAIAPHAS, a sleazy Southern judge

JUSTICE ONE, a lackey

JUSTICE TWO, a lackey

SERVANT GIRL, an L.A. fast-food server

PILATE, a gruff veteran soldier

THE OFFICER, a jaded policewoman

THE PLACE
On the road, somewhere

THE TIME
Now

Scene One

The Beginning of the Gospel

Three Travelers

(Mark 1:1-3)

(In the darkness, a single NOTE [cue 1] hangs in the air. It becomes the sound of a distant TRAIN WHISTLE, then a train. Growing louder, coming at us, it roars past, the whistle howling. The sound begins to fade.

(Lights up on FIRST TRAVELER. She's carrying luggage. Handles are littered with airline, bus, and train tags. She's dressed for travel. The train's wind ruffles her hair and clothes, then settles.

(She's looking up at an old-fashioned signpost. The arrows point in all directions: JORDAN RIVER, JUDEAN DESERT, GALILEE, CAPERNAUM, GERASA, TYRE AND SIDON, NAZARETH, CAESAREA PHILIPPI, JUDEA, JERICHO, BETHANY, JERUSALEM, etc. The signpost works as a scene indicator, with arrows removed or replaced appropriately.

(FIRST TRAVELER turns to us. She's reading a map, folding it out, tracing routes. Her finger stops on something. She smiles, pleased. She takes out a hand-held tape recorder and clicks it on.)

FIRST TRAVELER *(into recorder):* This is where it begins. The Gospel of Jesus Christ, the Son of God.

>   *(She flaps closed the map, stuffs it in a bag. She turns to go. Lights up on SECOND TRAVELER. He's sitting on two steamer trunks. A wooden folding chair leans against them. He's reading a Fodors tour book for Israel.)*

SECOND TRAVELER *(reading):* It's written in the prophets: "Look, I'm sending a messenger ahead to prepare the way. Listen, a voice cries out in the wilderness, 'Prepare a way for the Lord. Clear out a straight path for Him.'"

>   *(They look at each other. They push the trunks out of the way. Stack the luggage up neatly. The playing area is clear. They look up as . . .*

>   *(THIRD TRAVELER has come in, dressed in pale khakis and a hat. He looks like he's traveling on foot—tired and hot, with a backpack, satchel, and canteen. They all look at each other. A beat, then:*

(Blackout.)

Scene Two

The Baptism of Jesus

John the Baptist with Believers

(Mark 1:4-15)

(The sound of WATER [cue 2] rushing over rocks.

(Lights.

(THIRD TRAVELER is hunched down. He's pouring water from the canteen into a battered metal cup.

(SECOND TRAVELER is reading from the guidebook.

(FIRST TRAVELER is sifting through an open trunk.)

SECOND TRAVELER *(looking in index):* John . . . John . . . *(finds it)* John the Baptist. *(Flips to the page)* John the Baptist showed up in the desert. He preached a baptism of repentance for the forgiveness of sins.

> *(THIRD TRAVELER takes out a white cloth and dips it in the cup. Dabs his face, his neck, his arms.)*

> Crowds from Jerusalem and all over Judea flocked to see him. They confessed their sins, and he baptized them in the Jordan River.

> *(FIRST TRAVELER pulls out a giant overcoat, patched and tattered, and a worn belt. She helps THIRD TRAVELER get dressed. Ties the coat closed with the belt.)*

> John used to dress in a rough camel-hair coat. He wore a leather belt around his waist. He ate what he could find—locusts and wild honey. And he preached.

> *(THIRD TRAVELER has become JOHN THE BAPTIST, a wild-eyed street-corner preacher. Pulls a battered Bible out of the coat pocket. Waves it. Slaps it. Builds to a fury.)*

JOHN THE BAPTIST: Listen, listen, lis-TEN! He's coming SOON! Do you hear me? He's on His WAY! Someone much GREATER THAN I AM!

> *(He dabs the scarf in the cup and touches the face of FIRST and SECOND TRAVELERS—who have become believers.)*

> I'm not worthy! I am not WORTHY TO BEND OVER AND TAKE OFF HIS SHOES! Wa-TER! Just wa-TER! I'm baptizing you with water! But when He comes, He'll bap-TIZE YOU WITH THE HO-O-O-LY SPI-I-I-IRIT!

> *(Stops. A memory strikes him. A beat.)*

That's when He came to see me. From Nazareth in Galilee. I baptized Him in the river. The second He came out of the water, I SAW THE SKY FLY OPEN! The Spirit swept down on Him LIKE A DOVE! And I heard a voice from hea-VE-E-EN! "You are my beloved Son! YOU ARE MY DE-LIGHT!"

(JOHN THE BAPTIST *lets the cloth he's been holding unfold. It's a long white scarf, the onstage symbol of Jesus. He takes off "JORDAN RIVER" arrow. The next one reads "JUDEAN DESERT.")*

Immediately the Holy Spirit drove Him into the desert. He stayed out in the wilderness for 40 days, alone—except for the wild animals. The angels took care of Him.

(*He hangs the white scarf on the signpost, looks at it, then takes down "JUDEAN DESERT." The next arrow reads "GALILEE." Suddenly, he tears off his belt and roughly twists it around his wrists.)*

And after they'd arrested me, Jesus went to Ga-li-LEE! AND PREACHED THE GOSPEL! *(Fiery)* "The time has COME! The kingdom of God is NEAR! Repent and BELIEVE THE GOOD NE-E-EWS!"

(Blackout)

Scene Three

The Calling of the Disciples

Peter

(Mark 1:16-20)

(A FOGHORN [**cue 3**] *bellows, with the sound of the ocean and sea gulls.*

(Lights.

(THIRD TRAVELER comes in. Pulls a trunk away from the others. Takes out a pea coat or yellow slicker, with stocking cap. Puts them on.

(He becomes PETER, an old-salt stevedore, with brusque Brooklyn accent.)

PETER *(to us):* Ah . . . went somethin' like this. I looked up for some reason, an' I seen 'im walkin' along the lakeshore. He catches sighta me 'n' Andy—that's my brother, y'see—tossin' this net into the lake. Cuz at the time we was fishermen! Anyways, He shouts out to us. He says, "C'mon! Follow Me! I'll put ya to work fishin' for human people!" *(He laughs.)* Well *(snaps his fingers)*, we dumped the nets, and we're like ducks in a row! We keep walkin' up the beach awhile. Pretty soon we see Jimmy and John—the Zebedee brothers—sittin' in their boat mendin' their nets. Jesus sends up a shout to 'em, and they dump *their* nets and leave Pop in the boat with the hired help! *(A beat)* So now we're all followin' Jesus.

(He rubs his chin, chuckling at the memory. The lights fade to:

(Blackout.)

Scene Four

Healing the Demoniac

Peter

(Mark 1:21-28)

(MUSIC [cue 4]. Chaotic synthesizer. Disturbing.

(Lights.

(PETER is looking up at the signpost. He takes off "GALILEE." Next is "CAPER-NAUM." He turns to us, looking uncomfortable about something.)

PETER: So . . . we go to Capernaum. Saturday mornin' gets here, and we all head off to the synagogue, see, and Jesus starts in teachin'. Everybody's completely blown out a the water by what He's sayin', understand, cuz He talked like He had authority. Not like the lawyers and priests and all. All a sudden there's some guy with a demon! He starts screamin', "Why're You botherin' us, Jesus a Nazareth? Did Ya come here to destroy us? I know who You are . . . THE HOLY ONE A GO-O-O-OD!" And Jesus says to him, "That's enough! Get out a him!" And the demon throws the guy on the floor. He's jumpin' and shakin' . . . and the demon comes out a him with a shrie-e-e-ek! *(Lets out a breath)* We all looked at each other and we said . . . , "In church?" *(A beat)* "What kinda new religion is this anyways?" we said. "What kinda power's He got? He even gives orders to evil spirits, and they obey 'im!" Didn't take long. The word about Jesus was all over town.

(Blackout)

Scene Five

Healing of Peter's Mother-in-law

Peter's Mother-in-law

(Mark 1:29-34)

(Lights.

*(*PETER*'s napping against one of the trunks.*

*(*FIRST TRAVELER *comes in. She opens a trunk and puts on a white hotel robe and thick Harlequin glasses. She becomes Peter's* MOTHER-IN-LAW, *a nice older Jewish lady.*

(She drops the trunk lid loudly. PETER *wakes up. He sees her. Looks nervous.)*

MOTHER-IN-LAW *(Yiddish accent):* They all left synagogue. So where does Peter decide to shlep them all for dinner? *(To* PETER*)* His mother-in-law's house!

*(*PETER *smiles sheepishly. He leaves quickly.* MOTHER-IN-LAW *watches him go. Sighs.)*

Tell you the truth, I remember I wasn't feeling so hot. I was warm. Maybe a little fever. Ay-yay-yay! OK, I'm close to death! And my brilliant son-in-law decides to tell the Rabbi all about it! *(Surprised)* And he came in to see little me. He took hold of my hand. He lifted me out of bed and—gevalt!—the fever was gone. *(Snaps)* Like this! *(A beat)* So I got up and made them all a nice soup.

*(The sound of a CROWD [*cue 5*] gathering. Getting louder.* MOTHER-IN-LAW *looks around, uncomfortable. She pulls her robe tight around her.)*

By that evening, the whole city has set up house in front of my door! All of them with sicknesses—and possessed by the evil spirits. The Rabbi went out and touched every single one of them! And they were healed! Gesundheit. And He cast out the demons—but listen, He told the spirits all to hold their tongues! This Rabbi? They knew exactly who He was.

(Blackout)

Scene Six

A Postcard

Third Traveler

(Mark 1:35-39)

(A flashlight switches on.

(THIRD TRAVELER *is writing a postcard.)*

THIRD TRAVELER: "Greetings! Early. Sun not even up. Jesus off in a quiet place. Praying. Peter et al. found Him. 'Everyone's looking for you!' He said, 'Let's go to other towns so that I can preach. That's what I came here to do.'"

(Thinks a moment. Writes.)

"Will be traveling in Galilee preaching and casting out demons. *(A beat)* Wish you were here."

(He turns off the light.)

(Blackout)

Scene Seven

Healing of the Leper

Leper with Doctor and Photographer

(Mark 1:40-45)

(MUSIC **[cue 6]**. *Haunting minor piano, broken riffs. Then it becomes the sounds of a hospital—machines beeping, intercom voices, respiration.*

(Lights.

(FIRST TRAVELER *has become* **THE LEPER**. *She's sitting on the end of a trunk, a suitcase next to her. She has the white robe on backward, like a hospital gown. She looks drained.*

(SECOND TRAVELER *has become the* **DOCTOR**. *White coat. Holds a bottle of water upside down above* **THE LEPER**—*an IV. A clipboard in the other hand. Shows no emotion.)*

21

THE LEPER (*nervous at first*): The disease. I'd been infected with it. I found Jesus. I remember I fell down in front of Him. And I begged Him, I begged Him for healing. I said, "If You want to, You can make me well." He looked at me. I can still feel His compassion. He said, "I do want to." Without a second thought, He . . . He touched me. "Be well again." I *felt* the disease . . . leave my body—immediately. I was healed. "Don't tell a soul about this," He said. He was very serious about that. "Let them examine you. Then make an offering as proof of your health."

(*The* DOCTOR *is amazed. Looks at the clipboard. Takes out the IV in dismay.*

(*She yanks off the robe and hands it to him.*)

But the moment I checked out, I told anyone I saw the good news!

(THIRD TRAVELER *becomes the* PHOTOGRAPHER. *Old-style crumpled fedora. Takes a photo of her.*

(*She freezes in the flash. Hand in the air and a huge grin. Then she drops her arms. Remorse.*

(*The* PHOTOGRAPHER *runs off.*)

After that, I was told Jesus couldn't publicly enter a city anywhere in the country. He was forced to live out in deserted places. But people still came to Him from every direction.

(*Blackout*)

Scene Eight

Healing of the Paralytic

Paralytic with Buddy

(Mark 2:1-12)

(*MUSIC* [**cue 7**]. *'60s acid rock.*

(*Lights.*

(THIRD TRAVELER *has become the* PARALYTIC, *sitting in the wooden folding chair, very still, looking forward intensely. It's clear he's disabled.*

(SECOND TRAVELER *becomes* BUDDY. *He comes in wearing a sports jacket. Carries an army jacket with American flag patches and a baseball cap. He stops and puts the "CAPERNAUM" arrow on the signpost, then dresses* PARALYTIC *in the costume. Pats him gently and sits.* PARALYTIC *shows no reaction.*)

PARALYTIC *(a beat):* A few days later, Jesus found himself back in Capernaum. Word got out the Man was back home—and, of course, the crowds rushed the place. You couldn't get a foot in the front door. *(Bitter smile)* Standin' room only. And He started layin' the Word on 'em. Four of my buddies decided they were gonna . . . take me along for the ride. *(He looks at* BUDDY.*)* I told 'em, "Give it up! We're not gettin' in ta see Him. Don't you get it? It's packed in there!"

(BUDDY *cracks up.*)

So these nutcases carry me up on the roof! They break a hole in the tiles right above Jesus and lower me down on a stretcher smack in front of the Man!

(They laugh together for a moment. A beat. PARALYTIC *fights back emotion.)*

Jesus looked at me. At us. He could see how strong we believed. He said, "Son, your sins are forgiven."

(Struggles with the power of the moment. Shakes his head.)

But some of those great leaders of ours were there and heard Him say this. They got all bent out a shape about it. "Who does this Man think He is, forgivin' sins? Is He God?" Jesus looked right at them. Could read their minds or somethin'. "Why's this eatin' at you?" He said. "What's easier for Me to say to this man? 'Your sins are forgiven'? Or, 'Get up, take that stretcher, and go home'?" *(Beat)* Then He—man, I'll never forget this— He said to them, "I want you to understand that I have the power to forgive sins in this world." Then He turned to me. "Stand up. Grab that stretcher and go home." *(A beat)* And I—stood—up!

(PARALYTIC *shakily stands. His* BUDDY *goes to help. He waves him back. He proudly snaps the chair closed.)*

I grabbed that stretcher and *walked* out of there in front of them all! The place went nuts! Everyone started praisin' God. *(Shouting)* "WE'VE NEVER SEEN ANYTHING LIKE THIS BEFORE!"

(Blackout)

Scene Nine

The Calling of Levi

Levi

(Mark 2:13-17)

(The sound of a 10-KEY MACHINE [cue 8].

(Lights.

(SECOND TRAVELER has become LEVI. An overachieving, excitable nerd with a goofy chortle. Conservative jacket and tie. Thick glasses. Pocket protector. Working on a 10-key. A pile of 1040 forms near. Looks at a form. Shakes his head. Looks at another.)

LEVI: None of this adds up!

(Sees us. Stops. Becomes professional, restrained.)

Yes, well, once again Jesus found himself down by the lakeshore. The crowds, of course, gathered there to hear Him. And He . . . taught a seminar. As He was walking along, He saw me—Levi, the son of Alphaeus, as it were—sitting in the . . . well, the tax collection office, actually—

(Offstage BOOS and hisses [cue 9]. LEVI *looks off.)*

Look, it's a job! *(To us, restrained again)* Jesus leveled His gaze at me and said, "Levi, follow Me." *(Pause)* Well, I . . . how should I put this? I—

(Explodes over the trunk with a whoop)

I blasted off my backside and followed Him! *(A spasm of chortles)* I mean, what would you do, I must say!

(DINNER PARTY sounds [cue 10]—*voices, dishware clanking, music.* LEVI *gets restrained again.)*

So I invited Jesus for a little dinner party over at my townhouse. He was sitting there with all my friends—sinners . . . tax collectors . . . sinners— there were many who followed Him! Be that as it may, when the Pharisees—I have no idea *who* let *them* in—saw Him sitting there eating with the sinners—and the tax collectors—they said, "How can He eat with the scum of the earth?" Well, I must say! But Jesus heard them. He looked right at them and said *(excited)*, "It is not the healthy who need a doctor, but the sick! I have not come to call righteous people but sinners to salvation!" *(Beat)* AND TAX COLLECTORS!

(Blackout)

Scene Ten

Questions About Fasting and the Sabbath

Construction Worker and Boomer

(Mark 2:18-27)

(A montage of MORNING TV [**cue 11**] *show sounds—news, cartoons, game shows, "Good Morning America," etc. Someone remoting quickly.*

(Lights.

(FIRST TRAVELER has become a CONSTRUCTION WORKER. Bulky jacket. Hard hat. Lunchbox. Typically gruff. Sitting on one trunk, eating a Twinkie and drinking coffee. Reads the newspaper.

(SECOND TRAVELER has become the BOOMER. White robe. Slippers. Slicked-back hair. Glasses. Typically snobbish. Sitting on a trunk with coffee mug and box of Granola cereal. Reading the newspaper.)

CONSTRUCTION WORKER *(reads headline):* "Jesus Questioned About Fasting." *(Looks at the Twinkie. Shrugs. Continues reading.)* "Recently Jesus of Nazareth was asked by local religious authorities why He and His disciples never went on fasts, since this was the custom of other denominations—most notably the Disciples of John and *(a sneer)* the Pharisees." *(He freezes.)*

BOOMER *(reads the headline, horrified):* "Jesus Lord of the Sabbath?" *(Reads)* "Last Saturday Jesus and His disciples were seen walking through a grainfield plucking heads of grain and eating them." *(He looks up. Shocked.)* "Pharisees questioned Jesus on the subject, reminding Him what He was doing was not lawful on the Sabbath." I should say not! *(Freezes)*

CONSTRUCTION WORKER *(reading):* "'Are you asking the Bridegroom's friends to refuse to eat anything at the wedding while He's with them?' Jesus replied to the religious leaders." *(Laughs)* "'As long as they have the Bridegroom with them, there should be no fasting,' the famed Nazarene teacher went on to say." *(Bites the Twinkie)* "'But there will come a time when the Bridegroom will be taken away, and that will be their day to fast.'" *(He freezes. Puzzled.)*

BOOMER *(reading):* "'Haven't you heard about the time King David and his companions were starving?' the energetic Preacher from Nazareth replied to the authorities. 'He marched into the house of God and ate the sacred loaves of bread allowed only to the priests.'" *(Looks up, amazed. Freezes.)*

CONSTRUCTION WORKER *(reading):* "Jesus wrapped up the discussion by saying, 'No one patches old clothes with unshrunk cloth. The patch will rip away and make a bigger hole than before. And nobody pours new wine into an old wineskin. If they do, the wineskins break open, and both the skin and the wine is ruined! Fresh skins for new wine!'" *(Jumps up)* YEAH!

BOOMER *(reading):* "Jesus closed with this pronouncement: 'The Sabbath was made to benefit humanity, and not humanity to benefit the Sabbath. *(Wide-eyed)* Therefore, the Son of Man is ruler *even over the Sabbath!*'" *(Jumps up)* NO!

(Blackout)

Scene Eleven

Healing of the Withered Hand

Levi

(Mark 3:1-6)

(A PIANO [**cue 12**] *banging out "There Is a Balm in Gilead." Tinny.*

(Lights.

(LEVI is standing there with a hymnal.)

LEVI: We were in the service with Jesus. We all saw this man sitting there with a crippled hand. Everybody in the congregation was keeping their eye on Jesus to see if He would dare to heal the poor man on the Sabbath. So Jesus said to the man, "Stand up here in front of everyone." Then He turned to the congregation and He said.

(Suddenly explodes with excitement)

"What am I allowed to do on the Sabbath? Something good—or something evil? May I save a life, or destroy it?" But they sat there with their lips sewn shut! He gave them all that look—furious at their stupid, stubborn hearts. He said to the man, "Stretch out your hand!" *(He stretches out his hand.)* And he stretched it out—AND IT WAS COMPLETELY HEALED!

(A beat. Back to restrained.)

Of course, they all went out immediately and made plans to kill Jesus.

(Blackout)

Recorded Memories

First Traveler

(Mark 3:7-12)

(Lights.

(FIRST TRAVELER *comes in talking into the recorder.)*

FIRST TRAVELER: Wednesday evening. Today we went to the beach. Somehow everyone heard we were going to be there, and, of course, the place was packed. Crowds of people from Galilee, Judea, Jerusalem, Idumea. Some even came from as far away as Tyre and Sidon. Jesus asked us to have a boat ready, in case the people crowded Him into the water. Well, He'd healed so many, everyone was rushing at Him to touch Him. Every time someone possessed with a demon saw Him, they'd fall down and scream, "You are the Son of God!" But He kept telling them to be quiet. And to not reveal who He was.

(Blackout)

Scene Thirteen

Appointment of the Apostles

Peter

(Mark 3:13-19)

(Lights.

(PETER *sitting there, looking at a Polaroid photo. He smiles, remembering something.)*

PETER: Jesus hiked up into the hills, and He called some a us up there with Him. The ones He wanted. And He picked 12 a us, callin' us apostles—so we could be with Him, see, and He could send us out to preach, and give us authority to cast out demons and what have ya. Anyways, like I said, He picked 12—*(looks at the photo)*. Lessee, there was me—He gave me the name Peter then, see. Yeah. And there was Jim and John, the Zebedee boys. You remember them. He nicknamed 'em both the "Sons a Thunder"! OK, there's Andy, a'course! Yeah, and . . . Phil, Bart, Matt, Tom, Little Jimmy, Thad, Simon the Zealot! *(Sees a face. Sours.)* And Judas Iscariot. *(Stuffs the photo in his pocket)* The one who betrayed Him.

(Blackout)

Scene Fourteen

Jesus Accused of Insanity and Satanism

Mary

(Mark 3:20-30)

(MUSIC [**cue 13**]. *Sorrow theme: aching and sparse.*

(Lights.

(FIRST TRAVELER becomes MARY. She comes in, takes a faded cardigan sweater out of her suitcase. Pulls it on. Turns to us. There's a lot of pain here. And protective pride. A little shy at first.)

MARY: Someone or other had invited Him to their home. And the crowd started collecting outside the door. So many of them pushing in to see Him. No one inside was even able to eat supper. Word got to His family about it. And we decided we would all go down and take Him out of there. Because . . . *(this hurts)* because they were saying my Son was out of His mind! *(A beat)* But the lawyers and religious leaders were already there. All the way from Jerusalem. They started telling everyone He was possessed by Satan! Possessed? My Son? Did you ever hear such a thing? *(Imitating them)* "He can cast out demons because He's the ruler of demons!" That's what they said! *(Beat. She takes a breath.)* So He told them all a story. *(A beat)* "How can Satan drive out Satan?" He said. "If a kingdom divides up against itself, that kingdom will not last. If a house takes sides against each other, that house will never stand. And if Satan is fighting against himself, he will never survive. His kingdom is about to end. No one can walk into the home of a muscleman and steal everything he owns. First of all, he has to tie up the man, doesn't he? Once that's done, he can take anything he likes." *(A beat. She proudly smiles. Then serious.)* "Here's the truth," He said. "No slander is beyond God's forgiveness. But the person who slanders the Holy Spirit will never be forgiven. He has committed an eternal sin." *(A beat)* Well, you understand why He said that, don't you? It's because they said He was possessed by an evil spirit!

(Blackout)

Scene Fifteen

Jesus' Family
Mary
(Mark 3:31-35)

(The sound of a CROWD [cue 14] building. The sound continues through the scene.

(Lights.

(MARY is trying to see over heads. Standing on tiptoes. Looking around people. She turns to us, exasperated.)

MARY: We ended up outside the house, trying to get in where He was teaching. We finally sent a message in to Him, telling Him to please come out and talk to us. Someone inside said to Him, "Your family's waiting outside to see You." *(This hurts.)* He said, "Who is My mother? Who is My brother or sister?" And He looked around at all the people sitting around Him. And He said, "You are My family now. Whoever does God's will is My mother, My brother, and My sister."

(MARY feels the pain of this a moment.

(THIRD TRAVELER becomes JESUS. He comes in, goes to the signpost, and takes the white scarf. Kisses it like a stole. Puts it on.

(JESUS turns to MARY. Smiles at her.

(The CROWD [cue 14] comes up. Building. Insistent. Filling up the space between them. She reaches her arms out to Him.)

(Blackout)

Scene Sixteen

Travel Diary

Second Traveler

(Mark 4:1-2)

(CROWD continues through the scene.

(Lights.

(SECOND TRAVELER *is sitting on a trunk. Writes in his travel diary.)*

SECOND TRAVELER: Sunday afternoon. Late. *(Looks up)* Very cloudy. We were all walking along the beach. Jesus was teaching us. Suddenly we realized there was a huge crowd surrounding us. *(Smiles)* Jesus found a boat. We pushed it out into the water, and He sat in it. The people were all smashed together on the beach. Right down to the water's edge.

(Opens the trunk, pushes it downstage. Looks up at the sky. It's getting stormy. He goes out. CROWD continues and lights fade to:

(Blackout.)

Scene Seventeen

The Parable of the Seeds

Jesus

(Mark 4:3-20)

(Lights.

(JESUS *is standing in the trunk—now a boat. He's a good storyteller. Acting out parts, gesturing, dramatic.*

(Lights go to evening colors during the scene.)

JESUS: Listen! *(He sits.)* A farmer decided it was time to sow some seed. Now, as he was scattering the seed, some of it landed on the road, and the birds swooped down and ate it up. Some of the seed struck rocky ground— where the soil was thin and hard. They sprouted quickly, but as soon as the sun came out, the blazing heat wilted them, and they died. They had no root. Some of the seed dropped into the thistles. The weeds sprang up and choked the new-grown plants. They produced nothing. But some of the seed fell into good soil, and they yielded an amazing crop! Thirty, 60, 100 times what was planted! *(A beat. He smiles.)* If you have ears to listen, then hear.

(He gets out of the trunk. It's getting darker.)

When we finally found ourselves alone, My disciples flocked around Me, asking what I could possibly mean by a parable about farmers and seeds. I said to them, "You've been allowed to know some of the mysteries of the kingdom of God. But to those outside, I tell everything in parables. That way they can stare and see nothing. They can listen and not hear a thing. Or else every one of them would turn to God and be forgiven."

(He sees they're getting confused. He smiles. Sighs. And sits.)

You haven't figured out the parable? How are you going to understand any parable? *(He taps His head.)* It's like this. The farmer is sowing . . . *(waits for an answer)* . . . the Word of God. Those on the road are people in whom the Word is planted. No sooner have they heard it than Satan comes along and snatches away the Word struggling to take root. Then there are those who catch the Word on rocky ground. They take it in with joy! But there's no root. As soon as trouble or persecution comes along, they wither and burn. Now others are like those who snare the Word in thistles and thorns. They hear it, but soon the shiny glamours of the world—wealth and the desire for things—rise up and choke the plants. So they yield nothing. But then there are those, like seed sown in good soil, who hear the Word and welcome it. They produce a bountiful harvest! Thirty, 60, 100-fold!

(The lights fade to:

(Blackout.)

Scene Eighteen

Parables About the Kingdom

Jesus

(Mark 4:21-34)

(THUNDER [cue 15]. *Distant. Rain begins.*

*(*JESUS *turns on a flashlight. He talks in the circle of light. It feels late-night intimate.)*

31

JESUS: Do you switch on a lamp, and then stick it under a basket? Or slide it under a bed? Don't you put it on a table where it can light up the room? Nothing is hidden that won't one day be exposed. Nothing in the dark that won't soon be brought out into the light. Listen to what I'm saying. The measure you deal out to people, that's the measure you'll get back— and even greater. So the ones who have, they'll get more. The ones who have nothing, even that will be taken away from them.

(Someone asks a question.)

The kingdom of God? The Kingdom . . . is like that farmer who planted the seeds. He goes to bed at night, and when he gets up in the morning, the seed has sprouted already. He has no idea how it happened. The soil produced the blade, then the head, then the grain. And once the crop is ready, he goes out with his sickle and brings it in.

(Looks around. Is He getting through?)

How can we picture the kingdom of God? What story can capture it? *(He thinks.)* It's very much like a mustard seed. That's one of the smallest seeds you can find, isn't it? But once it's planted, it grows up into a huge plant. So large even birds build nests in the shade of the branches. *(He stands. To us.)* These are the kinds of parables I told—as much as people were able to understand. I always used parables. And when I was alone with My disciples *(a smile),* I explained them all.

(He snaps off the flashlight.)

(Blackout)

Scene Nineteen

Jesus Calms the Storm

Levi

(Mark 4:35-41)

(Crash of THUNDER [cue 16]. Then wind.

(Lights.

(LEVI is standing in the trunk. He's holding up an umbrella, trying to stay calm. The "boat" is swaying.)

LEVI: It was much too late in the evening when Jesus said to us, "Why don't we go over to the other side of the lake." We all replied, "THE OTHER SIDE OF THE LAKE? ARE YOU—?" *(Stops. Gets control.)* So we took Him, just

32

as He was, in the boat. There were other boats all around us. We left the maddening crowd far behind.

(A crash of THUNDER. He looks at the sky, terrified.)

And all of a sudden—THIS RAGING STORM HIT US!

(The boat is now rocking. He's trying to stay standing. Getting seasick.)

Waves were beating against the boat! Water rushing in on every side! We were sinking! You might well ask where Jesus was in all of this? He was in the back of the boat. SLEEPING ON A PILLOW! "Rabbi! Rabbi!" we shouted. "Don't You care if we drown?" Jesus jumped up. He scolded the wind, and He shouted at the waves, "Quiet! Be still!"

(The storm sounds fade.

(LEVI slows to a stop. Sneaks a hand out from under the umbrella. All clear.)

The wind stopped. The water went dead calm. "Why were you so terrified?" He said. "Don't you have any faith?" Then we looked at each other. Amazed. And we said, "WHO IS THIS GUY? EVEN THE WIND AND THE WAVES OBEY HIM!"

(He looks up at the clouds.)

(Blackout)

Scene Twenty

Healing of the Gerasene Demoniac

Rancher

(Mark 5:1-20)

(MUSIC [cue 17]. Sparse country guitar.

(Maybe a single slide and harmonica.

(Lights.

(FIRST TRAVELER *has become the* **RANCHER.** *Cowboy hat, vest, piece of rope. One foot on the trunk. Coils the rope. Looks at us. Tips the hat back. Slow talker. A tough hombre.)*

RANCHER: Seen 'em crossin' the lake there. Strangers. Rolled up on the Gerasene shore. All of 'em stepped out onto the beach. *(Shakes her head)* Never knew what in the world hit 'em. He come screamin' out of the graveyard up yonder. A crazy man. Had what I reckon you'd call an unclean spirit. Lived up there with all the dead folk. Nobody could fence 'im

33

up. Even with a chain. Ain't for lack a tryin' neither. Many times as you can count, we shackled 'is bones up. He buckled the locks. Snapped the chains. No one was strong enough to break the poor devil. Not a soul.

(A single NOTE [**cue 18**]. *Haunting and eerie. Growing louder.* RANCHER *visibly gets the shivers.)*

You could hear 'im up there. In the hills. Night and day, howlin' like a coyote. Naked as a newborn. Cuttin' 'imself up with rocks. *(Pause)* But he seen Jesus comin', that's for sure. Caught sight of 'im down there at the lake and starts howlin' and screamin'. Breaks for 'im at full gallop. Buckles to 'is knees in front of 'im. Starts shoutin' at the top a his voice. "What d'You want with me, Jesus, Son a the Most High God? Stop torturin' me!" But Jesus was a step ahead. He was already orderin' the unclean spirit to hit the road. "Come out of that man!" He was sayin'. "What's yer name?" Jesus asked the spirit. "Legion!" the thing shouted back. "Legion, cuz there's a herd of us in here!" Then the demons start beggin' somethin' awful for Jesus not to drive 'em out of the country. That's when Jesus looked up and saw our livestock. Our hogs, feedin' on the hillside right over there. The demons start hollerin' at Jesus, "Send us into the pigs! Send us into the pigs!"

(The sound of swine HOOVES [**cue 19**] *beating.*

*(*RANCHER *gets furious at the sound memory.)*

And I'll be hanged if He didn't. Gave 'em the go-ahead, and those evil things jumped straight for our herd! Pigs went crazy! Busted fences. Broke loose for the water and drowned themselves. Two thousand head! We took off for town. Told everybody we seen what happened. A whole posse of 'em came out to see Jesus and the madman—now sittin' there, big as day. Dressed decentlike and in 'is right mind. Folks who saw the whole thing started tellin' the story of the demons and the dead pigs.

(Straightens up. Pulls the hat forward.)

That's when we told Jesus and 'is men to get out of town. They got themselves back in the boat. The feller who'd been possessed begged to go with 'em. But Jesus told the man to stay put. "Go home," He said. "Tell your people what happened to ya. Tell 'em how God's had mercy on ya." So the man ran off and made it a point to spread the story all over these parts. And all them that heard it was amazed.

(A beat. Coils up his rope.)

(Blackout)

Scene Twenty-one

Healing of the Bleeding Woman and Jairus' Daughter

Jairus

(Mark 5:21-43)

(MUSIC [**cue 20**]. *Very emotional, swelling theme.)*

(Lights.)

(SECOND TRAVELER *becomes* JAIRUS. *Conservative overcoat—London Fog or the like. A hat. Thick glasses. Briefcase. He's very nervous. Not used to giving a testimony. Stumbles over words. Gets lost. Startled by the intensity of his own emotion.)*

JAIRUS: I, ah, first thing . . . I remember there was a crowd on the beach when Jesus got off the boat. People immediately recognized me. I was a leader in the local synagogue at the time. I—oh, excuse me. *(A trembling smile)* My name is Jairus.

(A beat. He gets his courage together.)

I also remember thinking the, ah, crowd wasn't going to stop me. I pushed to get to Jesus. And I fell on my knees in front of Him. I begged Him. Over and over. I said . . . I said, "My little girl. Oh, my little girl is dying. Please . . . please, if You could come with and me and lay Your hands on her, I . . . I know she'll be healed and live." *(A sigh)* And He came with me.

(Picking up confidence)

There was a huge crowd pressing in all around us. And there was a woman there. She'd been suffering from hemorrhages for something like 12 years. She said the doctors had done everything they could for her, but she'd just gotten worse and worse. Hopeless. Anyway, she heard about Jesus, and she shoved her way through the crowd and touched the hem of His cloak. I think she thought, If . . . if I can just touch His clothes, I'll be healed. Immediately she felt the bleeding stop, and she knew inside herself that she was well. Jesus . . . He looked around. I suppose He knew healing power had gone out of Him. He looked around and said, "Who touched My clothes?" But the disciples said, "Rabbi, You can see for yourself the crowd swarming all around You! How can You ask who touched Your clothes?" But Jesus . . . He, ah, kept looking around for the one who had done it. And the woman, knowing full well what had happened to her, fell down at His feet and confessed the whole thing. And Jesus looked at her, and He said, "Daughter, your faith has healed you. Go in peace and be freed from your suffering."

(Pause. A hard moment.)

Well . . . ah . . . *(Deep breath)* As He was speaking to her, some people from my house came up to me. They said . . . they told me . . . that my little girl was dead. Why should I bother the Rabbi anymore about it? And I . . . I . . . tried to . . . *(Clears his throat. Fighting for emotional control.)* Ah . . . excuse me—

(He cries quietly for a moment. Gets control. Takes out a handkerchief and wipes his glasses.)

I'm sorry. I . . . *(a breath)* Jesus . . . He, ah, overheard what they had said too. He looked straight at me, and He said, "Jairus, don't be afraid. Just believe." And He took . . . ah, Peter, and . . . James and John, and we all went to my house. People were crying and wailing. Jesus walked into the house and said, "Why are you crying? The little girl isn't dead. She's just asleep." But they laughed at Him. And He threw them out of the house! Then He took my wife and me, and those disciples who were with Him . . . and we went in to where my little girl was. He walked to the bed. He took hold of her small hand. And He said, "Little girl . . . little girl . . . I'm telling you to get up!" *(A beat. A small smile.)* She got up. She started walking around the room! Then Jesus told us . . . ah, he told us not to tell anyone what had happened. *(He smiles.)* Then he asked us to get her something to eat.

(Takes a deep breath. Puts the handkerchief away. He walks off. Stops and changes the signpost to "NAZARETH."

(The lights fade to:

(Blackout.)

Scene Twenty-two

Jesus Rejected in Nazareth

Mary

(Mark 6:1-6*a*)

(MUSIC [**cue 21**]. *Sorrow theme.*

(Lights.

(MARY is reading a yellowed newspaper clipping.)

MARY: My Son came home. To Nazareth. The disciples—and the crowds—

came with Him. When the Sabbath came, He went to the synagogue to teach. Everybody listening was astounded by Him. "Where does this Man get all this? What wisdom's been given Him? What miracles are done by His hands!" *(This hurts.)* Then they said, "Isn't He a carpenter? The Son of Mary? Don't His sisters live in town? And His brothers—James, Joses, Judas, and Simon? He's just one of us!" And they were all highly offended by Him. "A prophet is honored everywhere," He told them, "except in his own hometown. And among his relatives. *(A beat)* And his own family." *(A beat)* After that, Jesus wasn't able to do any powerful miracles here—except lay hands on a few of the sick and heal them. Their lack of faith . . . *(searches for the word)* . . . amazed Him.

(Blackout)

Scene Twenty-three

A Postcard

Third Traveler

(Mark 6:6*b*-13)

(Lights.

*(*THIRD TRAVELER *is writing a postcard.)*

THIRD TRAVELER: "Greetings! Teaching in the villages now. J. sent us out in twos. Gave us authority over evil spirits! Took nothing—except walking stick. No bread, bag, money! No extra shoes, clothes! He said, 'Stay in one home. If not welcomed or listened to, shake the dust off your feet when you leave as a sign against them.' Been telling all to repent. *(Amazed)* Casting out demons! Anointing sick with oil and curing them! *(A beat)* Wish you were here."

(Blackout)

Scene Twenty-four

Herod Kills John

Herod and His Barber

(Mark 6:14-29)

(MUSIC [**cue 22**]. *Mobster mandolin theme.)*

*(*Second Traveler *has become* King Herod. *Smoking jacket. Cravat. A real Mafia type. His face is lathered up.)*

*(*Third Traveler *has become* Barber. *White apron and towel. He's shaving* King Herod. *The procedure makes telling a story difficult—and dicey.)*

King Herod: Jesus. He's a big noise around here. Some're sayin', "It's John the Baptist raised from the dead! That's why he's so powerful!" Others say, "It's Elijah!" And some say, "It's one'a the prophets!" I'll tell ya what I think. *(A beat)* "IT'S JOHN THE BAPTIST! THE ONE I BEHEADED! HE'S COME BACK FROM THE DEAD!" Ow!

(Looks at Barber *and the razor.)*

Watch it with that thing, will ya? *(Sighs)* All right, all right. I'll give ya the scenario, OK? I had John pulled in, understand? He was givin' me grief about marryin' my brother Philip's wife. "It's not lawful for you to have your brother's wife!" he kept shoutin'. It was . . . startin' to hurt my feelings. But Herodias? My wife? Now she was really cheesed at ol' John. She wants revenge. Wants me to off 'im on the spot! I . . . I can't do that, see. Cuz I'm . . . well . . . I'm—

Barber: Scared of him.

King Herod: Who asked you! I have a healthy respect for the guy. He's . . . he's what you call a holy man, understand? I'm givin' 'im a little . . . protection, that's all. Gotta admit it, though. When I listen to him . . . *(points to his head),* he messes up the old brain. But Herodias got her big chance, anyways. The old hen waited until my birthday, see. I throw this bang-up party! A stag party, if ya understand my thinking. All my guys're there. And some big men around town. Influential types.

(MUSIC [**cue 23**]. *Salome's rhythmic dance.)*

*(*King Herod *and* Barber *suddenly stop and stare. Watching someone dance. Their mouths drop open in amazed lust.)*

That's when Herodias's daughter slinked into the place. And she . . . da-a-a-a-anced.

Barber: That what ya call it?

KING HEROD: And she . . . pleased me. In fact, she pleased all of us, if I remember correctly. So I said to the girl, "Ask me for whatever ya want! Even if it's half my territory! It's yours, sweetheart!"

BARBER (dry): Brilliant.

KING HEROD: The little thing runs to her mother and says (falsetto), "What should I ask for?" And the old hen cackles (hissing), "The heeead of John the Bapti-i-is-s-st!" So she runs back to me. (Falsetto) "I want you . . . to give me . . . on a platter . . . the head . . . OF JOHN THE BAPTI-I-I-IS-S-S-S-ST!"

(Long beat. Gets control of himself.)

I was grieved by this, understand. But what am I gonna do? I ain't nothin' if it's not a man'a my word. And then there's all my guests. I couldn't refuse.

(KING HEROD watches the BARBER's razor come down to shave his neck.)

I sent one'a my men to do the job. He went and took John's head. Brought it to me like I ordered. On a platter. And I gave it to the girl. (A beat) AND SHE GAVE IT TO HER MOTHE-E-E-E-ER!

(A pause. He gets over it. Leans back for the shave.)

When John's people heard, they came and got his body and buried it somewhere. (To the BARBER) Hey! Be careful with that thing!

(Blackout)

Scene Twenty-five

Jesus Feeds 5,000 People

Thomas

(Mark 6:30-44)

(The sound of a CHEERING CROWD [cue 24].

(Lights.

(FIRST TRAVELER has become THOMAS. Jean jacket. Backpack with buttons like "Question Authority." John Lennon glasses. A college student. Poli-sci major.)

THOMAS: It was intense! We were all telling Jesus about our trip. What we'd done and taught and everything. And He goes, "Let's get out of here. Go someplace quiet and, y'know, chill for a while." I'm all for that! There were people everywhere—coming and going. We couldn't like eat or anything. So, we got in a boat and took off. But, a'course, gazillions of people saw us, and they ran ahead. Soon as we hit the beach, the place was already full-on standing room only. But Jesus starts feeling sorry for them, because they're like sheep without a shepherd or something, and He starts teaching. Meanwhile, it's totally getting dark—so we went up to Him, and we said, "Rabbi, it's totally getting dark, and this place is like out in the nowhere! Why don't You tell everybody to find a town somewhere and buy themselves something to eat." But He says, "Why don't you give them something to eat." And we're all, "I'm too sure! Like we're supposed to spend major cash and throw this huge picnic or something. No way!" So He goes, "How many loaves of bread do you have, Thomas? Go and find out." So we looked, and there's like, five loaves and two fish. So He tells all the people to sit down on the grass in groups of 100s and 50s. Unbelievable! And He takes the five loaves and the two fish, looks up to heaven, says grace, and starts tearing up the bread. Then He gives it to *us* to give to all the people. R-I-I-I-GHT. And He also divides up the fish for everybody. *(A beat. Amazed.)* And everyone ate until they were full. I'm not kidding! We picked up 12 baskets of leftovers! And the number of people who'd eaten . . . well, it must have been . . . *(pulls out a calculator and punches)* . . . FIVE THOUSAND! *(Pockets the calculator)* It was a party.

(Blackout)

Scene Twenty-six

Jesus Walks on Water

Thomas

(Mark 6:45-52)

*(MUSIC [**cue 25**]. Craig's song. Alternative rock.*

(Lights.

*(**THOMAS** is sitting on a trunk, looking through CDs. Sees us.)*

THOMAS: After the bread-and-fish gig, Jesus tells us to go on ahead of Him in the boat to Bethsaida while He says good-bye to everyone. After that, He, like, went up into the mountains to pray or whatever. So, it's night now, OK?

(Sits on a trunk as if it were a boat. Rows.)

We're out in the middle of water, and He's alone on land, right? He can see we're struggling with the oars, cuz the wind's totally against us. So, about three o'clock in the morning, Jesus comes out to us. *(Astounded)*

Walking—on—the—lake! I'm too sure! We're all freaked out, because we thought He was, like, a ghost or something. And He's all, "Don't be afraid. It's Me." And He gets into the boat . . . and the wind dies down. And we're full-on amazed. I mean, we didn't even understand about the loaves yet! Our minds were like . . . closed. Y'know?

(Blackout)

Scene Twenty-seven

Travel Diary

Second Traveler

(Mark 6:53-56)

(Lights.

(SECOND TRAVELER walks in. Changes the signpost to "GENNESARET." Sits and writes in his travel diary.)

SECOND TRAVELER: "Thursday. *(Looks up)* Clear. Early morning. We docked at Gennesaret. Hadn't stepped off the boat yet when people rushed us. All around. Bringing the sick on mats. They follow us wherever we go. It doesn't matter if we go into villages or cities or farms; they even stretch the sick out in the marketplaces. Then they beg to touch just a piece of His clothes. Everyone that touches Him is healed."

(Blackout)

Scene Twenty-eight

Jesus Dispels Empty Traditions

Jesus

(Mark 7:1-23)

(Lights.

(JESUS is taking plates and cups out of a trunk as he speaks.)

JESUS: It caught the attention of some of the lawyers and priests who had come down from Jerusalem that My disciples were eating their food with "unclean" hands. That is, hands that have not been properly washed. They teach that you shouldn't allow a scrap of food to touch your lips unless the hands have been thoroughly and ritually washed. And so they take care to observe the traditions of the elders. They don't eat anything from the market unless they ritually wash it first. They have stack of other traditions like these. How one should wash cups, pots, kettles, and beds. So the priests were rankled by what they saw. *(A censorious voice)* "Why are your disciples eating with unclean hands? Can't they at *least* observe the traditions of our people?"

(A beat. A breath.)

Isaiah was certainly right when he wrote about you hypocrites: "These people honor Me with their mouths, but their hearts are miles from Me. They worship Me in emptiness, because they teach human rules as if they were doctrine." Don't you understand? You have let the commandments of God slip through your fingers while you grip traditions of your own making! Look, didn't Moses say to honor your father and mother? Whoever speaks evil against his parents should die? Then you turn right around and tell people it's perfectly fine to turn a deaf ear to a starving mother and a needy father and tell them, "Sorry, all my money goes to God." You crush the Law of God under your feet so that you can make a stand on man-made traditions! You do this kind of thing all the time.

(Turns to everyone. Angry.)

Listen to Me. All of you! Nothing going into your bodies from the outside is going to make you unclean. You do that well enough by what comes out of your mouths.

(Sits down. Rubs His face. A beat.)

I went inside after that, and My disciples came up to Me and asked what I meant by the parable. *(Looks up)* Parable? You mean, you didn't understand what I said? *(A breath)* Don't you see that nothing you eat is going to defile you? Doesn't it just go into your stomach and pass out of your body? It's what comes out of people that defiles them. It's from inside—from the human heart—that sinful intentions make their appearance. Promiscuity, theft, murder, adultery, greed, malice, deceit, indecency, envy, slander, arrogance, . . . and foolishness. All these things fester within. They make a person unclean.

(Looks at the piles of dishes and cups on the trunk)

(Blackout)

Healing of the Gentile Woman's Daughter

Gentile Woman

(Mark 7:24-30)

(The sound of RESTAURANT [cue 26] *chatter, dishware, bad Muzak.*

(FIRST TRAVELER becomes the GENTILE WOMAN. Wearing an ugly downscale restaurant apron. Hair pulled back. Looks haggard.)

GENTILE WOMAN *(comes in calling off):* Make sure you clean under those tables!

(Sees the signpost. Rolls her eyes and changes it to read "TYRE." Picks up the dishes and cups on the trunk. Sees us.)

I'd heard He was in the area. He'd gone to someone's house. Didn't really want anyone to know He was in town. But He could be found. If someone really wanted to find Him. *(A beat)* My daughter had . . . she had a demon inside of her. The minute I heard about Him, I knew I was going to Him for help. I bowed at His feet. And I begged Him to release her of this . . . thing. This spirit. He knew right away I was a gentile. Wasn't one of His people. He looked at me. "Haven't you heard, 'Let the children be fed first. It's not fair to take the children's food and throw it to the dogs'?"

(A pause. It hurts a moment. Then a smile. Understands the satire.)

I came back at Him. I looked Him in the eye and said, "That's true, Sir. But even the dogs under the table get to eat the children's crumbs!" *(She laughs.)* I think He liked my answer. "Go home," He said. "The demon has left your daughter." I rushed home. She was lying in her bed. Quiet. The demon was gone.

(Someone yells, "Order up!" She swipes her hair back and goes. Stops to change signpost to "DECAPOLIS." Lights fade to:

(Blackout.)

Scene Thirty

Healing of a Deaf Man

Jesus

(Mark 7:31-37)

(A series of TONES [cue 27]. High and low end, in between. Loud and faint. Like a hearing test.

(Lights.

(JESUS is standing there.)

JESUS: We left Tyre, went through Sidon down to the Sea of Galilee, and then into the Decapolis area.

(JESUS uses sign language as He speaks.)

Some people brought a man to Me. He couldn't speak. He couldn't hear. They begged Me to touch him, to heal him. I took him away to a private place, away from the crowd. I put My fingers in his ears. I touched his tongue with My saliva. I looked up to heaven. I sighed to heaven. Then I said, "Be open!"

(CROWD sounds [cue 28]. Distant, but growing louder.)

Immediately his ears were opened, and he could speak clearly. I told the people not to tell anyone what had happened. But the more I asked them to keep it quiet, the more they spread the news. Everyone was amazed beyond reason. "He does everything well!" they said. "He can even make the deaf hear and the mute speak!"

(CROWD continues to build as the lights fade to:

(Blackout.)

Scene Thirty-one

The Feeding of 4,000 People

Thomas

(Mark 8:1-9*a*)

(The CROWD [cue 28] sound swells.

(Lights.)

THOMAS: I couldn't believe it. People everywhere! AND NOBODY BROUGHT A LUNCH! *(A beat)* AGAIN! So Jesus called us over and dropped it on us. "I feel sorry for all these people." *(Aside)* Surprise, surprise. "They've been listening to Me for three days, and they've had nothing to eat. Some of these people have come a long way—if I send them home like this, they're going to pass out on the road somewhere." Yeah? SO WHY DIDN'T THEY BRING ANY BURGER BUCKS? Anyway, we said, "Tell us how we're supposed to feed all these people out here in the middle of nowhere." "How many loaves of bread do you have?" *(A beat)* I was afraid He was going to ask that. We counted up. "Seven." Same routine. He gets everybody sitting on the grass. Says grace, breaks the bread, tells us to give everybody dinner. OK, no problem. Someone had a couple of fish. Little guys. Jesus says grace for those, and He tells us to pass them out. Anybody got a guess what happened? Seven baskets of leftovers! Well, that's because this time there was only . . . *(punches on the calculator)* . . . 4,000. No big deal.

(Grins. The lights fade to:

(Blackout.)

Scene Thirty-two

Yeast of the Pharisees

Thomas

(Mark 8:9*b*-21)

(Lights.

(THOMAS is changing to signpost to "DALMANUTHA.")

45

THOMAS: Jesus sent the 4,000 off without dessert, and we got into a boat and went to Dalmanutha. That's where we ran into some establishment types again. They wanted a meaningful dialogue with Jesus. Actually, they just wanted Jesus to give them a sign from heaven. Thunder or something. It was a test, y'know? True or false. Use a number two pencil. This majorly upset Jesus. "How many signs do you need?" He said. "I refuse to give you another one!" And we storm off and get back into the boat and sail back to the other side. *(Smiles)* I think we passed the audition. *(Sits on a trunk)* So we're sitting there. Suddenly I realize I'm hungry. But we only had one loaf of bread in the boat. WHAT IS IT ABOUT FOOD AROUND HERE? Jesus suddenly turns and says, "Watch out for the yeast of King Herod and the priests." *(Does "Twilight Zone" theme)* We were massively confused. We thought He was just ticked because we only had one loaf of bread with us. Jesus figured out what we were thinking and gave us one of His looks. "Why are you talking about bread? Don't you get it? Are your hearts closed up? Are you blind? Are you deaf? Do you all have amnesia? When I divided up the five loaves for the 5,000, how many baskets of left-overs did you pick up?" Ummmmm. *(Starts to go for the calculator. Stops. Counts on fingers.)* Uh, 12. "And just now, the seven loaves for the crowd of 4,000, how many baskets then?" Ummmmm. Seven. Then He shoots us another look. Shakes His head. Then He said *(a beat)*, "Get a clue."

(THOMAS *changes the signpost to read "BETHSAIDA." He looks back at us. Shrugs.)*

(Blackout)

Scene Thirty-three

Healing of the Blind Man

Jesus

(Mark 8:22-27*a*)

(JESUS *speaks in the darkness.)*

JESUS: We stopped in Bethsaida. Some people brought a blind man to Me. They begged Me to touch him. I took him by the hand and led him out of town. I put saliva on his eyes and laid My hands on him. I asked him "Can you see anything?"

(JESUS *lights a match. His face can be seen. His shadow large on the walls.)*

He looked up at Me. "I think I can see people," he said. "They look like . . . trees walking around."

(**JESUS** *blows out the match. Darkness.*)

I laid hands on his eyes again. He opened them. Stared hard for a moment. And his eyesight came back to him.

(Lights)

He saw everything clear as day. Then I sent him back home. I warned him, "Don't stop in town and talk about this."

(He changes the signpost to read "CAESAREA PHILIPPI.")

We went on to the towns around Caesarea Philippi.

(Blackout)

Scene Thirty-four

The First Prediction of the Passion

Jesus

(Mark 8:27*b*—9:1)

(NIGHT sounds with crickets [**cue 29**].

(Lights.

(Evening. **JESUS** *sits on a trunk near a "fire." He "stirs" the embers. Thinks a moment.)*

JESUS: On the way to Caesarea, I asked My disciples . . . *(Looks at them; a beat),* "Who do people say I am?" *(A beat. Uses voices.)* "Some say You're John the Baptist. Some say You're Elijah. Others say You're just one of the prophets." *(Stirs the fire a moment. To us.)* "What about you? Who do *you* say I am?" *(A beat)* It was Peter who answered this time. He said (**PETER'**s *voice),* "YOU ARE THE CHRIST!" *(Smiles fondly. Then serious.)* So I warned them not to tell *anyone* who I was. And I began to explain to them how I would suffer, and be rejected by the priests and the teachers of the law—and that I must be killed.

(Stands, hands up as if quelling a reaction.)

I told them the bitter truth—and Peter took Me aside, and he began to scold Me, and I said, "Out of My sight, Satan! *(A beat. Softer tone.)* Peter, you're not thinking like God now, you're thinking like a man!"

(That hurt. Takes a deep breath. Turns to us.)

Listen to Me. If any of you wants to become My follower, you must drop your self-absorbed living, shoulder your cross, and follow Me. If you try to save your life, you will lose it. But if you will lose your life for Me and

47

the gospel, you will save it. What do you gain by getting your hands on the whole world—and losing your own soul? What can any of you give in exchange for your soul? If anyone is ashamed of Me and My words in this sinful, unbelieving generation, I will be ashamed of him when I return in God's glory with the holy angels. I'll tell you the truth, there are some standing here now who will not taste death until they see the kingdom of God arrive in power.

(Blackout)

Scene Thirty-five

The Transfiguration

Peter

(Mark 9:2-13)

(MUSIC [**cue 30**]. *Ethereal, "Heart of Space" sound.)*

(Lights.

*(*PETER *is there.)*

PETER: Almost a week later, Jesus decided He wants to take me and Jim and John and do a little mountain climbin'. Just the three of us. While we were up there, He . . . *(loss of words)* . . . I don't know how to say this. Jesus starts to . . . change in front of us! Transfigure, that's the word! His clothes, they start . . . glowin'. Brighter than St. Elmo's fire! And while this is happenin', we see two men talkin' with Jesus. I'm sure it was—I know this is hard to swallow—but it was Elijah and Moses! There I said it. They're talkin' to Jesus plain as day. So I opened my big mouth. "Hey, Rabbi, it's good we came along, huh? We can throw up three tents. One for You, and Elijah there, and Moses." I mean, what else am I s'posed to say at a time like that? I was scared spitless! Then a cloud rolls over the whole shebang, and we hear a voice. "This is My precious Son! Listen to Him!" So later—after we opened our eyes—we see the whole thing's a done deal, and Jesus is standin' there by himself. *(Takes a breath. Shakes out his head.)* So we start climbin' back down the mountain, and Jesus warns us not to tell anybody what we'd just seen. Until after He'd risen from the dead—whatever that was s'posed to mean! *(Winces)* There I go, thinkin' like a man again! Anyways, we was talkin' among ourselves, tryin' to figure this whole thing out with Elijah and Moses. I asked Him, "Rabbi, why does everyone say Elijah has to come first before the Messiah?" He said to us, "You're right. Elijah's comin' to put everything in or-

48

der. Why do you think it was written that the Messiah would suffer and be treated like garbage? I'll tell ya somethin'. Elijah's been here. And they had their way with him. Just like it was written." *(Very confused. Looks at the audience.)* Go figure that one.

(Blackout)

Scene Thirty-six

Healing of a Demoniac Boy

Father

(Mark 9:14-29)

(MUSIC [cue 31]. Chaotic, unsettling, atonal.

(Lights.

(SECOND TRAVELER has become the FATHER. A heavy coat. Hard hat with a "Power Company" logo. Hard, New England accent. No nonsense. Very blue collar.)

FATHER: Looked like the whole world was there, it did. Priests and lawyers arguin' and shoutin' at the disciples there. That's when we all seen Him comin'. Down from the mountain. The people went nuts! Never seen anything like it. Everybody rushin' to grab Him. First thing He says is, "What's all this arguin' about here?" I shout out a the crowd, "Rabbi! I brought You my son here. He's got some kinda evil spirit! *(This is hard.)* Whenever this thing grabs hold of him, it . . . it throws him to the ground, and he starts foaming at the mouth like an animal. His teeth chatterin'. What's more, he's gettin' worse every day. I gave him to Your disciples here to get it out, but it's no use." Hoo, boy. He got hot. "You faithless generation. How long will it be before you believe? How much longer am I supposed to put up with you? Bring the boy to Me." And they showed Him my son. When the evil spirit saw Jesus, it threw my boy to the dirt. He starts rollin' around, foamin' at the mouth. Like always. Jesus turned to me. "How long has he been like this?" *(Chokes back tears)* "Since he was a kid, Rabbi! How many times that evil thing has pushed him in the fire or the water to kill him. Oh, please! Please! If You can do anything, have a heart and help us!" Jesus looked right at me. *"If* I can help him? Everything is possible for the one who believes." I didn't know what to say. I started crying, right in front of Him there, I did. "I believe," I said. "O God! Help my unbelief!" Jesus looked around. Rubberneckers were pilin' up everywhere. So quick He looked at my boy and said, "You deaf and mute spirit! I command you, come out a that boy and never enter him again!" My . . . son started screamin' at the top of his lungs. It was awful! Shakin' and rollin' in the dirt. Then he stopped dead. He wasn't movin'. I . . . I thought the thing had finally killed him! We all thought that. But Jesus grabbed his hand and pulled him up. *(Amazed)* And he stood there. He did.

(**FATHER** *gets up to leave. Remembers something.*)

When Jesus went inside, I heard His disciples askin' Him why they couldn't cast out the demon. He said, "This kind only comes out with prayer."

(Doesn't understand this. Smiles and shrugs. The lights fade to:

(Blackout.)

Scene Thirty-seven

Another Prediction of the Passion

Thomas

(Mark 9:30-32)

(Lights.

(**THOMAS** *comes in. Changes the signpost to "GALILEE." Sees us.*)

THOMAS: Road trip! This time through Galilee. Now, He didn't want anyone to know where we were, cuz He was teaching us all.

(Takes out a spiral notebook to take class notes.)

That's when He told us again. *(Reads)* "The Messiah is going to be betrayed into the hands of men. They'll kill Him. But three days after His death, He'll rise from the dead." *(Looks at the notes. Shakes his head.)* Look, we totally didn't understand a word of what He was talking about. And we were all, like, too afraid to raise our hands and ask Him.

(Blackout)

Scene Thirty-eight

Jesus Talks About Greatness

Little Child with Jesus

(Mark 9:33-38)

(MUSIC [**cue 32**]. *Non-nursery children's theme.)*

(Lights.)

(JESUS *is sitting on the trunk.)*

(FIRST TRAVELER *has become* LITTLE CHILD. *Sweater around the neck. Popular lunchbox. Waves at* JESUS. *Pulls the chair up to the signpost. Stands on it and changes the arrow to "CAPERNAUM." Biting a tongue as she concentrates. Flounces to the trunk. Sits next to* JESUS. *Takes out a granola bar. Starts to eat. Breaks it in half and gives one to* JESUS.)

LITTLE CHILD: Jesus came back here. To *(sounds it out)* Ca-per-na-um. He was sleeping over at my house. All His friends too. I 'member He asked a couple of them what they were fighting about while they were walking. They looked scared when He asked that. Like they'd been bad or something. I found out they were fighting about which of them was the coolest. The greatest. Jesus said to them, "If you want to be really great, you hafta wanna help people." Right?

(JESUS *smiles and nods.)*

(LITTLE CHILD *giggles. Kicks feet.)*

Now this is the part where I come in. He called me over and sat me on His lap. He even put His arms around me, 'n' He said to everyone, "Anybody who accepts a little child in My name accepts Me. And anyone who accepts Me is accepting God, the One who sent Me here!" Right?

(JESUS *nods.)*

(LITTLE CHILD *smiles.)*

Then one a the disciples looked real mad. He told Jesus there was some guy casting out demons—but he told the guy to knock it off cuz he wasn't in their group. And he was right.

(Looks at JESUS, *who shakes His head)*

And he was not right. Right?

(JESUS *smiles.)*

(Blackout)

Scene Thirty-nine

Jesus Talks About Temptation
Jesus with a Little Child
(Mark 9:39-50)

(Lights.

*(*LITTLE CHILD *is lying on the trunk. Face in hands. Watching* JESUS.*)*

JESUS: No one who exercises power in My name is going to turn against Me easily. Anyone not against us is for us. This is the truth of it: if anyone so much as gives you a cup of water because you belong to Me, they won't go unrewarded.

(He looks at LITTLE CHILD. *Something is bothering Him. A flash of anger.)*

If any one of you—any *one* of you—pushes My little ones into sin, it would be better for you if someone had tied a boulder around your neck and pushed you into the lake.

(A beat. He thinks. He whispers something in LITTLE CHILD's *ear. He's telling the child to leave the room. The child doesn't want to. Hurt, pleading, finally flouncing off.* JESUS *turns to us.)*

Listen to Me. If your hand is forcing you to sin, chop it off. It's better to live forever one-handed than have two hands to point you into hell. And if your foot walks you into sin, cut it off. It's better to be disabled than to have two good feet to run you into damnation. And if your eye keeps you in disgrace, gouge it out. It's better to be half-blind than have perfect vision and see the place of burning, where the conquering worm never dies, the flames never go out, and where everyone is salted with the blaze. *(A beat)* Salt. Salt is good, isn't it? But if it loses its saltiness, how are you going to season it again? Don't lose your seasoning. Treat each other well.

(The lights fade to:

(Blackout.)

Scene Forty

Jesus Questioned About Divorce

Lawyer

(Mark 10:1-12)

(MUSIC [cue 33]. *Classic theme, Bach-ish.)*

(Lights.)

(FIRST TRAVELER becomes LAWYER. Hair up. Hip glasses. Conservative blazer. Briefcase. She breezes in. Checks Dayrunner "To Do" page. Looks irritated for having forgotten something. Stalks over and changes the signpost to "JUDEA." Checks watch. More irritation.)

LAWYER: Jesus was scheduled for some meetings in Judea beyond the Jordan. *Pro bono* work. As per usual, there were unforeseeable delays. Namely, every time people showed up, Jesus felt the need to stop and give a seminar. Finally, the lawyers and priests got in touch with Him. We had a . . . legal question we wanted a consultation on.

(Opens the briefcase. Takes out a file.)

"Yes, uh . . . Mr. Christ. Do You think it's legal for a man to divorce his wife?" "What does Moses have to say on the subject?" He counters. Oh, He's good. *(Looks in a huge tome)* "Well, he said it was perfectly legal for a man whenever he wants to write out a divorce certificate and get rid—ah, to . . . dismiss his wife." So He decides to set precedent. He says, "Moses made that ruling because of your hard hearts. But I'm telling you—from the beginning, God made them man and woman in order for the man to leave his father and mother to be united with his wife. They're no longer a two. Now they're a one. No one should separate what God has joined together. *(A beat)* If a man divorces his wife in order to marry another woman, he's guilty of adultery against her. *(A beat)* The same goes for a woman."

(LAWYER is stunned. Slams the tome closed with a loud thunk.)

(Blackout)

Scene Forty-one

Jesus Blesses the Children

Mom

(Mark 10:13-16)

(The sound of CHILDREN [cue 34]. They're playing, laughing, shouting, squealing.

(Lights.

(FIRST TRAVELER has become MOM. A heavy autumn coat. Scarf. Slight Southern accent. Holding a small jacket. At the park, trying to spy her child.)

MOM *(calling a child):* Timmy!

(Holds up the jacket for him to come get it. Looks at us. Smiles.)

We all brought our children down to see Him. We were kind of hoping He would, you know, lay His hands on them and give them a blessing of some kind. *(Calling)* Timmy! *(To us)* Anyway, the disciples really got mad about it. They tried to stop the kids. The minute Jesus saw what was going on, He got real—well, let's just say He did not approve of the disciples' behavior. "Let the children come over here to Me," He shouted at them. "Stop holding them back. God's kingdom belongs to every one of them!" Then—I'll never forget this—He said, "The person that refuses to come to God as a little child will never be allowed in the Kingdom." Isn't that great? Then the kids went rushing at Him. He took every single one of them up into His arms, laid His hands on them, and blessed them. *(A beat. Calling.)* TIMOTHY JOHN, I MEAN NOW!

(Blackout)

Scene Forty-two

The Rich Man

Rich Man

(Mark 10:17-22)

(The sound of a TRAFFIC JAM [**cue 35**]. *Honking, squealing tires.*

(Lights.

(SECOND TRAVELER has become RICH MAN. Italian suit jacket, sunglasses. Sitting on a trunk, like the front seat of a car. Talking on a car phone.)

RICH MAN: I said sell! SELL! *(About to hang up. Softens.)* Make sure you give 10 percent to the Widows and Orphans Fund. No, wait—15. Yeah, yeah, ciao.

(Hangs up. Looks irritated at the traffic. Picks up the phone again. About to dial. Sees us.)

Jesus decided He was going out on another publicity trip. I happened to catch Him just before He left.

(Dials the car phone. Hits the breath spray. Someone answers.)

Oh, Good Teacher. Rich Man here. Listen, I'd like You to fill me in on something? What must I do to get a handle on this eternal life thing. *(Listens)* Uh-huh. Oh, I see. *(Covers the phone)* He asked me why I called Him good. He said no one's good except God alone. *(On phone)* Uh-huh. Sure. Uh-uh. Gotcha. *(Covers it)* He said, "You know the commandments, don't you? Don't murder, commit adultery, steal, lie, cheat; but have respect for your father and mother." *(On phone)* Rabbi, Rabbi . . . You're preaching to the choir here. I've kept all those commandments since I was old enough to have a paper route. *(Covers it)* Well, I have! *(A beat)* That's when I felt something from Him. It was . . . I knew He loved me. *(On phone)* Wait . . . no, I . . . You don't under . . . Rabbi . . . *(A beat. To us.)* He said there's still something I can't count among my assets. I . . . I have to sell off everything I own . . . and give the money to the poor. Then I'll have . . . treasure in heaven. Then He told me to follow Him. *(A beat)* I'm . . . I'm shocked. I—I'm hurt, that's what I am. He doesn't understand! I'VE GOT A LOTTA STUFF!

(Slams the phone down. Stunned. Then sad. Turns on the radio. We hear the NIGHTLY BUSINESS REPORT [**cue 36**].*)*

(Blackout)

Scene Forty-three

Jesus Talks About Treasure

Jesus

(Mark 10:23-31)

(The NIGHTLY BUSINESS REPORT [**cue 36**] *continues.*

(Lights.

*(*JESUS *is sitting on the trunk.)*

JESUS: "How hard it will be for those who have wealth to get into heaven." *(Smiles)* This completely shocked My disciples. That's why I said it again. "Children, do you know how difficult it is for people who trust in their money to get into heaven? It's easier for a camel to squeeze through the eye of a needle than for the wealthy to enter heaven." Of course, this amazed them. They asked each other, "If the rich can't be saved, who can?" *(A beat)* "Listen, for human beings this is impossible, but not for God. God can do anything." Peter stood up and shouted (**PETER**'s *voice),* "Look, we've left it all behind to follow You!" *(He smiles.)* This is a promise. No one who has left home, or family, or parents, or children, or careers for My sake and the sake of the gospel will go unrewarded. You'll receive 100 times more in this life, including homes, brothers and sisters, mothers and children—along with persecution. And in the age to come —eternal life. *(Leaning in)* Many of the people who seem so important now? They'll be last in eternity. And the least here, they'll be the greatest in heaven.

(The lights fade to:

(Blackout.)

Scene Forty-four

The Third Prediction of the Passion

Jesus

(Mark 10:32-34)

(MUSIC [cue 37]. Sorrow theme.

(Lights.

(JESUS is sitting there. PETER's pea coat and stocking cap lying on the trunk.)

JESUS: We were on the road. *(Smiles)* Again. This time heading for Jerusalem. I walked on ahead of everyone. I could feel it behind Me. The terror and anxiety about what would happen in the city. I stopped and took the 12 of them aside with Me. *(A beat. A deep breath.)* "You can see we're going to Jerusalem. There I'll be handed over to the leaders of the people, and they will condemn Me to death. They will then give Me to the Romans—who will mock Me, spit on Me, beat Me,—and kill Me. But after three days I will rise again."

(Stands. Puts His hands up to calm them. Shush them. Goes to the signpost. Takes off "JUDEA." The only arrow left reads "JERUSALEM." The signpost now makes a perfect cross.)

(Blackout)

Scene Forty-five

The Request of James and John

Peter

(Mark 10:35-45)

(Lights.

(PETER is staring up at the signpost cross.)

PETER *(not taking his eyes off the sign):* "Teacher, we're gonna ask You for somethin'—and we wanna make sure You say yes." (JESUS' *voice)* "Whaddayou want Me to do for you?" "We want You to fix it so we can sit next to You on big thrones when You make it to heaven."

57

(A beat. Turns to us.)

Wait a minute! I don't want you thinkin' *I* asked a question like that! Nah . . . it was the Zebedee boys. Johnny and Jim. They were always goin' off half-cocked. Anyway, Jesus said to 'em, "You don't know what yer askin' Me. You think you can drink from the cup I'm gonna drink from or be baptized with the baptism I soon will be?" They said, "We can." *(Shrugs)* Not a bad answer. Then He said somethin' strange. "Yer gonna drink the cup I'm drinkin'," He said. "Yer gonna be baptized just like I'll be." Then He told them to just get the sittin'-on-thrones business out a their heads. Those seats a honor were already reserved. Well, I'll tell ya the truth. When we heard that the Z brothers'd tried to horn in on the good stuff, we got pretty hot. Jesus felt the tension, all right. He called a group meeting.

(He sits. Teaches like Jesus.)

"There're powerful people in this world who just love to lord it over everyone! That's not the way it's s'posed to be with you guys. If one a you gets it in his head he wants to be great, he better start by bein' a servant. I didn't come here to be served, but to serve. *(A beat)* And to give My life as a ransom . . . for many."

(**PETER** *is astounded and pained by these last words. He wrestles with them as the lights fade to:*

(Blackout.)

Scene Forty-six

Healing of Blind Bartimaeus

Bartimaeus

(Mark 10:46-52)

(STREET [**cue 38**] *sounds. Crowds, cars, machinery. Then a voice is heard. Calling from the aisle.)*

BARTIMAEUS: JESUS! SON OF DAVID! HAVE MERCY ON ME! JESUS SONOF-DAVID! JESUSONOFDAVID!

(Lights.

(**SECOND TRAVELER** *has become* **BARTIMAEUS**. *Dressed like a street person. Dark glasses. A white cane. A grungy fast-food cup for change. Loud, obnoxious, and endearing. Thwacks his cane along the chairs, excusing himself. Grabs an audience member's arm.)*

You know where you are? You're in Jericho, in case you don't know! I was sitting over there on the curb *(swings the cane wildly)*, plying my trade as a . . . small-change operator! *(Laughs)* That's when I heard the news! Jesus of Nazareth's in town! *(Calling)* "JESUSONOFDAVID! Have mercy on me!" The people standing around started telling me to shut my grungy mouth! But not me! I turned up the volume! "JESUSONOFDAVID! HAVE MERCY ON ME!" Then Jesus stopped—I *heard* Him, OK! And He shouted out, "Bring him over here!" Yikes! The crowd changed their tune in a hurry. Now it's all "Hey, He's calling you," and "What a lucky guy!" I jumped up and ran right to Him.

(BARTIMAEUS starts one way, then another. Licks a finger and holds it up. Nods and walks to "Jesus.")

"What do you want Me to do for you?" He asked me. I said, "Rabbi, I want to see again!" He said, "Then go—your faith has healed you!"

(Takes the glasses off. Cautiously. The bright light burns the eyes. Covers them. Then looks at own hand. Then hands. Then clothes.)

I received my sight. And now I'm following Him! *(Calls)* Hey, wait up!

(Throws down the cane, glasses, and cup. Starts running down the aisle.)

Jesus! Wait up! Hey! Hey! JESUSWAITUP!

(Blackout)

Scene Forty-seven

The Triumphal Entry

Two Tourists

(Mark 11:1-11)

(A PARADE [cue 39]. *Distant drums, whistles. Marching music. People cheering.*

(Lights.

(FIRST TRAVELER has become TOURIST ONE. Angels baseball cap. Ugly windbreaker. Hard Midwestern accent. Looking through binoculars. Obviously excited.

(THIRD TRAVELER has become TOURIST TWO. Angels cap. Gaudy shirt. Midwestern accent. Holding a camera. Shades his eyes, craning to get a better look.)

TOURIST ONE *(without looking at* TOURIST TWO*)*: Heard a great story. Wanna hear it?

(TOURIST TWO shrugs "OK.")

They were right outside the city, OK? Near the Mount of Olives. You got the picture? He sends two of His disciples into one of the outskirt towns. He tells them, "Go on into that little town over there. You'll find a colt tied up. No one's ever ridden it. Untie it and bring it back with you. And if anyone says, 'Hey, just where do you think you're going with the horse?' You just tell them I need it and'll get it back to 'em soon." Did you catch that? Did you get that?

*(*Tourist Two *shrugs.)*

Well, lo and behold, they found the colt just like He said. They untied the little guy, and just then some of the bystanders asked the $20,000 question, just like He said they would. So they turned around and told 'em what Jesus told 'em to say. And they let 'em go. Boom. Like that. Incredible.

(Band and cheering continues.)

Tourist Two: What's going on? I can't see!

Tourist One *(through the binoculars):* Amazing! That's incredible! Never seen nothin' like it!

*(*Tourist Two *grabs the binoculars and looks through them. Problem is—* Tourist One *is still wearing them.)*

Tourist Two *(through the binoculars):* There He is! He's near the city! People've thrown their jackets on the colt! He's riding it! People are throwing their jackets on the road! Some are throwing down branches! This is great! It's a parade! People are shouting something!

Tourist One *(gagging out):* Hosanna!

Tourist Two: What?

*(*Tourist One *yanks the binoculars back. Says the next lines looking through the binoculars.)*

Tourist Two: They're saying, "HOSANNA!"

Tourist One: Blessings on the One who arrives in the name of the Lord!

Tourist Two: Blessings on the One who restores David's kingdom!

Tourist One/Two: HOSANNA IN THE HIGHEST!

Tourist One *(through the binoculars):* He's in the city now! He went straight to the Temple! He's looking around at everything! Looking! Looking! Still looking! *(A beat)* He's gone.

Tourist Two: What?

(Grabs the binoculars. Same bit as before.)

He's gone! He's . . . walking toward Bethany. With the rest of His group. *(Looks up.)* It must be too late. The party's over.

(They look at each other. Sad.

(The lights begin to fade.

*(*TOURIST TWO *motions for them to squeeze together. Holds the camera at arm's length. They smile. As the lights go out, the flashbulb goes off:*

(Blackout.)

Scene Forty-eight

A Postcard

Third Traveler

(Mark 11:12-14)

(Lights.

*(*THIRD TRAVELER *is writing a postcard. It clearly says, "Jerusalem.")*

THIRD TRAVELER: "Finally here! Strangest thing happened today. Outside the city, Jesus got hungry. Saw a fig tree. Bare. Just leaves. No figs. Jesus cursed it. 'May no one eat fruit from you ever again.' Very strange. It's not fig season yet." *(A beat)* "Hope to see you soon!"

(Blackout)

Scene Forty-nine

The Cleansing of the Temple

Carny Man

(Mark 11:15-19)

(MUSIC [**cue 40**]. *Merry-go-round organ.*

*(*SECOND TRAVELER *has become* CARNY MAN. *Shiny, threadbare, '40s suit jacket. Grimy, porkpie hat. Gloves with fingers gone. Creepy. Hands on three shells and a coin on a trunk.)*

CARNY MAN: C'mere. Got something to tell ya. Closer! That's good. Keep yer eye on the money, eh?

(Starts the shell game. Darts the shells around.)

They were here. Him and the rest of His troupe showed up here at the Temple. Are ya watching? *(Stops)* Here? *(Picks up a shell. Empty.)* Ahhh. *(Starts moving)* So they're all here. People excited. An event! What's He do? He throws everyone out! Any soul buying or selling something gets his backside kicked out of the Temple! Crack! Over go the tables of the money people! Smash! Tumble goes the tables of the vendors selling worship accoutrements! Puts His big foot down, Jake. No one in or out with anything! *(Stops)* Where is it? Here? *(Picks up a shell. Empty.)* Ahhhh. Too bad. *(Starts moving)* "MY TEMPLE SHOULD BE A HOUSE OF PRAYER FOR ALL PEOPLE! YOU'VE TURNED IT INTO A THIEVES' PARADISE!" *(Laughs)* Hey, I resemble that remark! *(Stops)* Here? *(Nothing)* Ahhhh. *(Moving)* At sundown, Jesus and His troupe packed it up and left town. But the religious and civic community were not exactly grinning. They didn't want to touch Him because the folks just loved Him. He had 'em shaking. That was when they decided it was time for Jesus to . . . leave this earthly plane. *(Stops)* Here? *(Picks up a shell. There's a coin. Holds it up.)* Well, aren't you smart.

(Blackout)

Scene Fifty

A Postcard

Third Traveler

(Mark 11:20-21)

(Lights.

*(*THIRD TRAVELER *is writing on the "Jerusalem" postcard.)*

THIRD TRAVELER: "P.S. Passed by the same fig tree this A.M. It's withered to the roots. Strange."

(Blackout)

Scene Fifty-one

Jesus Talks About Faith and Forgiveness

Jesus with Thomas

(Mark 11:22-26)

(MUSIC [**cue 41**]. *Contemporary synthesized instrumental.*

(Lights.

(JESUS is sitting on the ground. THOMAS in a chair, taking notes. The "QUESTION AUTHORITY" backpack sticker in plain view.)

JESUS: Have faith. *(He smiles.)* In God. With faith you could tell this mountain to pull itself up and go jump in the sea—and if you believed in your heart that it would happen, it would be done for you.

(THOMAS raises a hand to ask a question.)

I'll say it again. Whatever you ask in prayer, believe you are receiving it—and it will be yours. *(A beat)* When you start praying, remember to forgive whatever you're holding against anyone. This way God can forgive your sins as well. If you don't forgive others, neither will God in heaven forgive your wrongdoing.

(THOMAS raises a hand, urgently.)

(Blackout)

Scene Fifty-two

Jesus Questioned About Authority

Thomas

(Mark 11:27-33)

(Lights.

(THOMAS jumps out of a chair. Excited.)

THOMAS: We were walking through the Temple, totally minding our own business, OK, when this bunch of suits and big-time authority types start coming off on us. Seriously. *(A voice)* "One question, Jesus! One question! Who gave You the authority to do the things You do?" Jesus wailed on 'em with this. "Let Me ask you just . . . one question. Give Me a decent

63

answer, and I'll tell you by what authority I'm in business. *(A beat)* John's baptism. Was it a heaven thing, or, like, did he make it up?" *(Laughs)* They all start bustin' veins over this one! *(Voices)* "If we tell 'im it was a heaven thing . . ." "He'll give it to us for not believing." "But if we tell 'im John made it all up . . . ?" "Everybody thinks John's a prophet!" "The people'll take us out. Word." *(The "Enterprise" computer)* "We need further data." *(Smiles)* So Jesus said, "Then I'm not going to answer your question." It was so totally great.

(Blackout)

Scene Fifty-three

The Parable of the Vineyard

Jesus and Levi

(Mark 12:1-12)

(MUSIC [**cue 42**]. *Sorrow theme.*

(Lights.

(JESUS is there. Full of emotion.)

JESUS *(to us):* Can I tell you a story?

> *(Grabs a chair. Sits backward in it. Casual.)*

There was a man who planted a vineyard. He threw up a fence around it. Dug a pit for crushing grapes and built a watchtower. Then he rented it out to some tenants and went on a long vacation. When harvesttime came, he sent one of his workers to collect his share of the crop. But the tenants grabbed his worker, beat him senseless, and sent him back empty-handed. So the man sent another worker. But the tenants treated him exactly the same. They humiliated him, beat him up, this time causing serious brain damage.

(It's becoming obvious this is not just a teaching parable. This hurts.)

So another worker was sent. This one they killed. But the man kept sending workers to collect what was his, and the tenants continued to beat them savagely. Or murder them. Finally the man was at his wit's end. He had only one person left to send. *(A beat)* His own son. He sent him to the tenants. "Surely they'll respect my own son," he said to himself. But when the tenants saw the son coming, they said, "Look, this is the heir! Let's kill him, and the inheritance will be ours!" So they grabbed him. And killed him. And threw his dead body out of the vineyard. *(A beat)*

Now, what do you think the owner of the vineyard will do? *(Waits for an answer.)* He will come and destroy those tenants—and give the vineyard to others. Well, haven't you read this scripture? "The stone the builders rejected has become the cornerstone. It's the Lord who has done this. Isn't it amazing in our eyes?"

(JESUS *freezes.*

(LEVI *comes in. Looks at* JESUS.)

LEVI *(to us):* The priests and lawyers wanted to arrest Jesus on the spot. But they were afraid of the crowds. So they left Him and went off. *(A beat)* They knew the story was about them.

(Blackout)

Scene Fifty-four

Jesus Questioned About Taxes

Levi

(Mark 12:13-17)

(Lights.

(LEVI *is digging in a pocket. Pulls out a coin. Looks at it a moment.)*

LEVI *(a little panicked):* Tax season is coming up! *(Lets out a breath)* Sorry, old habits. I remember they once came to Jesus with an inquiry of a fiscal nature. *(A voice)* "Rabbi, we know You're a very sincere man." That's how they framed the question. "We know You're not partial to anyone, but teach God's truth regardless of what anyone thinks." *(Aside)* Is anyone falling for this? "Do we have to pay taxes to the government or not? Should we pay or shouldn't we?" No, you don't have to pay—UNLESS YOU WANT TO GO TO JAIL! *(A beat)* Sorry, old habits. Anyway, Jesus saw they were trying to trick Him. "Let Me see a coin," He said. So they handed Him a coin. He looked it over. "Whose face is on this coin? Whose name?" And they said, "The emperor's." *(Exploding)* Then Jesus—oh, this is great!—He looked at them and said, "Well, then give the government what belongs to the government! AND GIVE TO GOD WHAT BELONGS TO GOD." Yes, yes, YES! I wish I'd thought of that. I could have used that one. *(A beat)* Sorry. Old habits.

(Blackout)

Scene Fifty-five

Jesus Questioned About Resurrection

Lawyer and Court Reporter

(Mark 12:18-27)

(A GAVEL [**cue 43**] *pounding. Someone calling, "Order! Order!"*

(Lights.

(The LAWYER *is there, huge books in hand. Questioning a witness. Courtroom histrionics.*

*(*SECOND TRAVELER *has become* COURT REPORTER. *Conservative blazer. Mimes typing the transcript.)*

LAWYER: Mr. Christ, am I to understand You actually believe in a resurrection? Well, I have the law right here. *Ex facto jus oritus,* hmmm? *(Opens the book)* Moses tells us clearly that if a man dies without children, it's legal for the man's brother to marry the widow and have children in his brother's name.

(Snaps the book closed. Dramatically thoughtful.)

Work with me on a possible scenario here, hmmmm? Let's say there were seven brothers. Now, the oldest brother gets married—and promptly dies. No children. Sad. So the second brother marries her, and soon he dies as well. Still no progeny. So the third brother enters into this fatal nuptial arrangement. Dead. No kids. And so on, et cetera, et cetera, et cetera. Soon, all of them have married her, and all of them have died, and none of these deadly unions produced a single heir! *(Aside)* Hey, it could happen! Finally, the woman herself falls into that eternal sleep. So, here's the question: When they all rise up on the final day, whose wife is she going to be, hmmm? I rest my case! Read that back to me.

*(*COURT REPORTER *clears his throat. Painfully shy.)*

COURT REPORTER: Ahem . . . yes, well. *(Reading from the transcript)* Then Jesus said, "I see the problem here. You have no understanding of Scripture and are completely unclear on the concept of God."

*(*LAWYER *gasps.*

*(*COURT REPORTER *looks around, nervously.)*

"When the seven brothers and the woman rise from the dead, they won't be married any longer. They'll be like angels. But that's beside the point. The real issue here is whether or not there is going to be a resurrection at all. Haven't you read in the book of Moses the story of the burning bush?

God said to Moses, 'I *am* the God of Abraham, I *am* the God of Isaac, and I *am* the God of Jacob.' Therefore, ipso facto, God is not the God of the dead, but of the living. *(A beat)* And you've made one big mistake."

(A beat. COURT REPORTER *breaks out laughing. Then sees* LAWYER *glowering.)*

*(*LAWYER *spins around on a heel and stalks out.* COURT REPORTER *sits there. Dazed.)*

(Blackout)

Scene Fifty-six

Jesus Questioned About Commandments

Court Reporter

(Mark 12:28-34)

(Lights.

*(*COURT REPORTER *runs downstage. Carrying a steno pad.)*

COURT REPORTER: Rabbi! Rabbi . . . ah, Sir. *(Gets up some courage)* I . . . ah, noticed how good You were in there. I was wondering *(trying to find the right phrasing),* well, if You could tell me which commandment is the most important one of all. *(To us)* He looked like He didn't even have to think about it.

(Opens the pad and takes dictation.)

"This is the first," He said. "'The Lord our God, the Lord is one. Love the Lord God with all your heart, with all your soul, with all your mind, and with all your strength.' And the second one is this, 'Love your neighbor as much as you do yourself.' There are no greater commandments than these." *(Amazed at the answer)* I . . . I couldn't believe what I said next. I looked at Him and I said, "You're right, Rabbi! . . . I mean, I think loving God as You say—and loving your neighbor as yourself—I . . . I think that's more important than all the sacrifices in the Temple put together!" Then He said *(looks at the pad, reads),* "You're not far from the kingdom of God." *(Awed)* That's what He said to me. *(A beat)* Well, nobody dared ask Him another question after that.

(Blackout)

Scene Fifty-seven

Jesus Talks About Hypocrisy

Jesus

(Mark 12:35-40)

(CROWD [cue 44] cheering. Loud.

(JESUS is there. Shouting over the crowd.)

JESUS: How can the lawyers argue that the Messiah has to be the son of David? Didn't David himself speak through the Holy Spirit and say, "God said to my Lord: "Sit at My right hand until I crush Your enemies under Your feet"? If David calls the Messiah "Lord," how can He be his own flesh and blood?

(CROWD getting louder. Out of hand.)

Listen to Me! Watch out for the lawyers and the teachers of the law! They love to walk around in their scholarly clothes and be lathered with respect when they go downtown. They demand the best seats in the synagogues and places of honor at banquets! But they swallow up the homes of widows and cover up their cheating with long-winded prayers! Because of this hypocrisy, their punishment will be all the worse!

(The CROWD cheers. It's deafening. Alarming.)

(JESUS rakes his eyes across all the faces. Are they listening anymore?)

(The CROWD fades out.

(JESUS stands there a moment.)

(Blackout)

Scene Fifty-eight

The Widow's Offering

Widow

(Mark 12:41-44)

(ORGAN MUSIC [**cue 45**]. *A hymn.*

(**First Traveler** *has become the* **Widow**. *Threadbare jacket. Worn fabric bag. Junk-drawer brooch. An elderly woman on Social Security.*

(**Second Traveler** *has become the* **Usher**. *Dark jacket. Appropriate tie. Censorious. Mimes passing a plate down the rows behind her.*)

Widow: I saw Him sitting across the room during the collection, watching the congregation put money in the offering. *(Looks around the "church")* A lot of well-off folks attending here. They can sure fill up a plate. *(She pulls a Social Security check out of her purse.)* First of the month. Payday.

(The **Usher** *comes by. She drops the check in the plate.)*

Doesn't amount to a penny, I'm sure. I remember I had just thought that —when I heard Jesus tell some of the folks sitting around Him *(whispers),* "This is the truth. That widow over there—struggling financially as she is—has put more in the offering than anyone here. The wealthy give out of their profits. She has given all she had to make ends meet." *(She shrugs. Smiles.)* Ends always seem to meet.

(The organ continues. The lights fade to:

(Blackout.)

Scene Fifty-nine

Jesus Talks About the End

Jesus

(Mark 13)

(ORGAN MUSIC continues.

(Lights.

(**Jesus** *is outside "church." Looking up at the building.)*

69

JESUS: After the service My disciples were amazed at how beautiful the building was. I said, "You see these walls? There's a time coming it will all be in ruins. Not a single stone will be left on top of another."

(JESUS *realizes the shock value of His words. Walks to another part of the stage.*)

We went to the Mount of Olives. Some of the disciples came and asked Me when this terrible thing would happen. Would it come without warning?

(*A beat. He sits. This is difficult. Like hard words about the world spoken to children. But He speaks them passionately. Urgently.*)

I don't want you to be led astray. There will be plenty who appear on the scene using My name and saying, "I'm the one!" Many will be seduced by them. When you hear the news about wars and rumors of wars, don't be afraid. The end is only near. Nation will rise up against nation. Country against country. There'll be earthquakes and famine everywhere. But these are just the contractions. The beginning of labor. (*A beat*) You are going to be in danger. When all this happens, you'll be dragged before courts, you'll be beaten in synagogues—you'll stand in front of governors and heads of state because of me. This is your chance to testify about the gospel. Don't worry about what you'll say when the moment of truth comes. The Holy Spirit will prompt your words. During that time, brother will betray brother to his death. Families will be ripped apart. Children will call for the murder of their own parents. Everyone will despise you because you belong to Me. But the one who endures to the end will be saved. Keep your eyes wide open. When you see the unholy sacrilege set up in the Temple, it's time to escape to the mountains. If you're on the roof, don't climb down to get something. If you're out in the field, don't run back to get your coat. How awful for pregnant women or the mothers of newborns in those days! Pray you won't have to make your escape during winter. You will see suffering around you more terrible than anything since creation. If God hadn't cut short the days, no one would survive. But for the sake of believers, the time will be endurable.

(*A beat. A breath. More hard words.*)

Listen closely. If *anyone* says to you, "Here is the Messiah!" or "There is the Savior!"—don't believe a word of it. False messiahs and phony prophets will rise up, manufacturing miracles and faking signs to control you. Be on your guard. You've been warned about it all. And when all the great suffering ends, then the sun will be eclipsed and the moon will lose its light. Stars will plummet from the skies. The heavens will begin to shake! Then you will see Me arrive in the clouds with power and glory. I will send out the angels to gather up the believers from the four corners of earth and heaven. Get your clues from the fig tree. When you see the branch is tender and the leaves begin to sprout, you know that summer is on its way. So you'll also know that I am nearby, waiting to return. I'll tell you the truth, this generation will not die before all this has run its course. Heaven and earth will disappear before My words fade. No one knows the day or the hour when all this will happen. The angels have no idea. And neither do I. Only God holds the appointment. So, keep sharp. You don't know when the moment will suddenly fall all around you. It's like a wealthy man who goes on a trip to another country. When he leaves, he puts his servants in charge of everything and demands his guards keep a lookout at the door. So stay awake. You have no idea when the Owner of the house will come home. Morning, noon, or night. You don't want Him to catch you asleep. What I'm saying to you now, I say to everyone. Stay sober. And awake.

(Blackout)

Scene Sixty

Anointing and Betrayal at Bethany

Judas

(Mark 14:1-11)

(MUSIC [**cue 46**]. *Intense, aching blues on sax.)*

(Lights.

(SECOND TRAVELER has become JUDAS. Leather jacket. Boots. Hair in a bandanna. Lying on the floor. Very strung out. Suddenly startles awake. Reaches for a mirror on the ground. Nothing. Wipes the glass with a finger. Rubs teeth. Looks around. Sees a newspaper. Reads the date.)

JUDAS: I can't believe it! It can't be only two days till the holidays! *(Throws the paper down. Suddenly laughs. Bitter.)* Those lawyers. Government people. They're still looking. Eyes peeled for a way to pop Jesus. Take Him out. Oh, but it's all very hush-hush. Back-alley deal. Shhhhh. *(Whispers)* "Not during the holidays. We don't want to cause a riot." Good thinking.

(Jumps up. A sudden thought. Angry. Starting to feel the addiction. Moving around. Disconnected.)

I couldn't believe . . . this is amazing! We were at Bethany. Simon the Leper's house. She comes in. This . . . woman. Breezes in with this alabaster jar of perfume. Incredible stuff. Pure. Probably cost an arm and a leg, you know. The fool breaks it open and starts pouring it on Jesus' head! I went off! "What're you doing? You're wasting good stuff! We could have moved that stuff fast and made a fortune on it. We . . . we could give it to our favorite charity!" Man, I let her have it. Right there. What a waste! We needed that! "Leave her alone, Judas!" He said. "Why're you giving her such a hard time? She's done a favor for Me. You'll always have the poor to show kindness to. You won't always have Me. Wherever the gospel is preached, what she's done today will be remembered. And honored. *(A beat)* She's just anointed My body for its burial."

(Feeling the pain now. The drive for a fix. Drops to the knees.)

Have to do something. Have to. *(Stops. Remembers.)* I went to them. *(Whispers)* "I know where He is . . . I can get Him for you." They grinned. Pumped my hand. A done deal. With the green attached. I just needed to stay sharp. Looking. Look. Look for the right time. To make the connection.

(Blackout)

Scene Sixty-one

The Passover Meal

Peter

(Mark 14:12-31)

(MUSIC [cue 47]. Classical guitar.

(Lights. Dim. Atmospheric.

(PETER sits on a chair behind a trunk. The Last Supper table. Obviously upset.)

PETER: It was finally Passover. I asked Jesus where He wanted to celebrate the holiday. He sent us into town. Told us to follow some guy carryin' a pitcher of water. When he gets to his house, we ask 'im where the room is. The one we're s'posed to set up for the Passover dinner. We did like he told us. Like always. We follow the guy. He shows us this huge room on the second floor. The place was already decked out for a party. I mean, all we had to do was . . . light the grill.

(DINNER [cue 48] sounds. Clanking dishware, talking, laughing. PETER "eats" for a moment. Looks around, trying to catch the other "disciples'" faces.)

It was pretty late. We were sittin' around the table with 'im. All'a us. Just eatin'. All'a sudden He comes out with, "One of you is going to betray Me. Someone eatin' at this table." Just like that! Well, I wasn't takin' that sittin' down! "Yer *not* talkin' about me?" I started yellin'. "A'course you don't mean me!" Then He said, "It is one'a you. One a you eatin' out'a the same bowl with Me right now." *(A beat. Fights the emotion.)* Then He tells us,

"I'm gonna die, just like it's been written about Me. But how sorry for the one who betrays Me! He'll wish he'd never been born!"

(A beat. Sighs. This is difficult.)

After that, we tried eatin' again. But Jesus takes up this loaf a bread. He looks up t' heaven. Says a blessin'. Then He starts passin' it around to all a us. "Take this and eat it, this . . . *(a deep breath)* . . . this is my body." *(Fights back emotion)* Yeah, so then He picks up a cup. He says a blessin'. And He starts handin' it around. And we all drank from it. He tells us, "Drink this . . . this is My blood. Blood of the new covenant, which is poured out for many. I won't drink wine again till I can drink new wine with you in heaven." *(Frustrated anger)* Then He starts tellin' us we're all gonna desert Him or somethin'! "The shepherd's attacked. Sheep scatter. After I've risen, I'll go ahead a you into Galilee." *(Stands)* "WHADDAYOU TALKIN' ABOUT? I don't care what these yahoos do! They can *all* take off on Ya! But I'll *never* desert You!" He says, "Peter, tonight before the rooster crows twice, you'll deny you even know Me three times." "No! NO! Even if I have to die with You, I'LL NEVER DENY YOU!" *(A beat. Bitterly.)* Never.

(Blackout)

Scene Sixty-two

Gethsemane

Jesus

(Mark 14:32-50)

(MUSIC [cue 49]. An emotional adagio.

(Light on JESUS.

(He's doubled over. Palms flat. Hurting. Feeling the emotion in His body. He pulls himself up on His knees.)

JESUS: We went to Gethsemane. I took Peter, James, and John aside. I wanted them to sit with Me while I prayed. I was trembling. Felt so terrified. Alone. "My soul is so heavy. I'm going to die. Stay awake with Me."

(Falls forward on His hands)

"Father . . . keep this terrible moment away from Me! It's all possible for You! Take this cup of suffering away from My mouth! *(A beat. Fights through it.)* No. Don't give Me what I want. Only what You desire." *(He sits up. Turns around.)* "Peter, are you sleeping? Couldn't you stay awake with

73

Me for one hour? Keep your eyes open. Pray. Keep out of temptation's way. The spirit is willing, but the body is so weak!" I went back to prayer. When I returned, they were all asleep again. They were so tired. None of them knew what to say to Me. It wasn't long. They fell dead asleep again. *(Stands)* "That's enough sleeping! Wake up. The time has come. I'm about to be seized by unholy hands. Get on your feet! Can't you see? *(A beat)* My betrayer is here."

(SIREN [cue 50], distant and wailing. Growing closer. Screeching. Red lights pulse the stage. JESUS faces them.)

They came at Me. A crowd with weapons and clubs. Sent from the authorities. *(This hurts.)* Judas was with them. He had arranged a signal with them. "The one I kiss," he said. "That'll be your Man. Arrest Him and take Him away—under guard." So he walked straight for Me. "Rabbi!" And he kissed Me.

(He rips off his scarf and roughly wraps up his wrists behind his back. Plays the chaos.)

They grabbed Me! Someone standing nearby started swinging a knife and hacked off an official's ear. *(Shouting)* "Am I a criminal? You've come out here with weapons and clubs to capture Me! I was with you every day in the Temple, and you didn't touch Me then! But the Scriptures must be fulfilled." *(A beat)* And they all deserted Me. And fled.

(The lights fade to:

(Blackout.)

Scene Sixty-three

Jesus Before the Council

Caiaphas and the Justices

(Mark 14:53-65)

(MUSIC [cue 51]. A thick, dark, and deep note. It builds for a few moments.

(Then voices arguing onstage. Heated. Outraged.

(Lights.

(FIRST and THIRD TRAVELERS have become JUSTICES. Black choir robes. Black masks. Gavels.

(SECOND TRAVELER has become CAIAPHAS. Hideous jacket. Hair parted down the middle. Huge gavel. Everything about him is huge. Stereotypical Southern senator at a kangaroo hearing.

(JESUS' *scarf lies crumpled on the floor.*)

CAIAPHAS: Judges. *(Pounds the gavel)* JUDGES!

> (JUSTICES *stop arguing. They look at* CAIAPHAS. *He bows his head.*)

> O Lo-o-o-oad. Bless what we's about ta do heh.

ALL: Amen.

CAIAPHAS *(histrionic):* Judges, the accused—Jesus a Nazareth—has been brought befo the Ha-a-a-ah Co-o-ourt! The priests, the elder statesmen, and the lawyers ahr awl assembled.

> (JUSTICE ONE *hands over a note. Reads.*)

> Ah understand the one theh cawl Peter is standin' outside the courtroom this vehry minute! Consortin' with the gawds and wawming himself by the fahre! Thank you, Judge.

> *(Pockets the note. Turns to the room.)*

> Now, we ahr lookin' for testimony this evenin'—*(checks his watch)* . . . excuse me, this early mownin', ta put this heh troublemaker to death!

JUSTICES *(pounding their gavels):* DEATH! DEATH!

CAIAPHAS: So fah we have found nothin'. Now, we have certainly had testimony awright. But none of them seemed to agree.

JUSTICE TWO *(reading):* One of the witnesses said, "I heard Him say He'd destroy this Temple made with hands and in three days build another not made with hands." And the other witness said—

CAIAPHAS: Thank you, Judge. We awl understayand the testimony did not agree!

> *(The big moment. He goes to "Jesus." Blustering.)*

> Haven't Ya'll got one word in Yo defense, Son? What about all these people testifyin' against You? Don't just stayand theh sayin' nuthin'! Ah'll ask You just one mo time, Sah! Tell us the truth! AWR YOU NOW OH HAVE YOU EVAH BEEN THE MESSIAH? THE SON A GAWD!" *(He gasps. Stumbles back.)* Did you heh that? Blasphemy! Heresy! Read that back!

JUSTICE TWO: The accused said, "I am. And you will see Me sitting at the right hand of the Power and coming with the clouds of the sky!"

CAIAPHAS: Why do we need to cawl any furthah witnesses? You have heard the incriminating filth from His vehry lips! What is yo' verdict!

JUSTICES *(pounding their gavels):* DEATH! DEATH!!

CAIAPHAS: The ayes have it! We fahnd You deservin' of death!

> (CAIAPHAS *snatches up the scarf, viciously. The* JUSTICES *pound their gavels on the lid of the trunk. A driving, steady beat.*)

75

Then some a us spit on Him! And we slapped His face! And we yelled, "Prophesy!" And the gawds took Him. And theh beat Him.

(The pounding continues. The lights fade to:

(Blackout.)

Scene Sixty-four

Peter's Denial

Servant Girl

(Mark 14:66-72)

(MUSIC [cue 52]. A rap beat. Driving. Angry.

(Lights.

(FIRST TRAVELER has become SERVANT GIRL. Funky, gaudy uniform top. Silly hat. Works in a fast-food chicken place. Drinking Coke from a fast-food cup. Listening to a Walkman—the rap beat we hear. Nodding her head.

(JESUS' scarf lies in a heap on the ground. She sees us. Pulls off the Walkman. The beat cuts out.)

SERVANT GIRL: I work down here in the courtyard. It's a OK job. Anyways, that's where I seen 'im. Peter. That his name? Yeah. He's trying to get warm over there at the grill. Looks lost, y'know. I'm lookin' at him really hard. Starin' right at him. "You're with that Jesus, the guy from Nazareth, right?" But he totally denies it. He goes, "Don't know 'im at all. Got no idea what you're even talking about." Then, I hear this rooster crow somewhere, and he gets all white. And he walks away. Now, see, I'm sure it's him. So I start asking around some of the other customers. And I finally say, "Oh yeah. That's him. I'm sure of it." But he totally denies it. Right to my face. Then one of the other customers chimes in. "I know you're one of those disciples, pal. Besides, you're from Galilee. I can tell." And so this guy Peter gets all hyped and starts cussing at us. "I swear I don't even know who you're talking about!" Then it happened again. That rooster crowing. And he turns white again. His face looks like he's remembering something. I don't know. Anyways, he started crying. Right there. Covered his face and bawled like a baby.

(She thinks about his face a minute, then shrugs. Pulls the headphones up. Drinks her Coke.)

(Blackout)

Scene Sixty-five

Jesus Before Pilate

Pilate

(Mark 15:1-15)

(MUSIC [cue 53]. Military snare.

(Lights.

(Early morning colors. SECOND TRAVELER *has become* PILATE. *Strides in with a limp. Army field jacket. Helmet with stars stuffed under his arm. Walks with a cane. He's the archetypical command general, gruff and aloof. He stops at the scarf, still lying in a crumple. Stiffly picks it up. Squints at us.)*

PILATE: At 0600 hours, they secured the prisoner. Led Him away. Deposited Him at my command.

(He walks around "Jesus." Looks Him up and down.)

"So tell me—are You the King of the Jews?" I asked. "You have said it." That was all I could get out of the Man. Then those infernal lawyers started braying and barking about this crime and that. *(Holds up his hand for quiet)* I asked Him again. "Aren't You going to answer me? Do You hear the charges they're bringing against You?" But he was as tight-lipped as a POW. I was amazed. *(A beat)* At that time, I was in the habit of releasing one prisoner during the Passover festivities. People's choice. I had a bad one locked up, I remember. Murderer. Rabble-rouser. Name: Barabbas. The crowd asked me to do for them what I usually did. I said, "Do you want me to release to you the King of the Jews?" *(Flash of anger)* I knew it was out of envy that they had handed Him over to me! But the priests whipped the crowd up in favor of Barabbas. So I said, "What do you want me to do then with the one you call King of the Jews?" And they shouted at me: "Crucify Him! Crucify Him! CRU-CI-FY HIM!" *(Losing his command)* And I said, "Why? WHY? What wrong has the Man done?" But they shouted all the more, "CRU-CI-FY HIM! CRU-CI-FY HIM! CRU-CI-FY-Y-Y HI-I-I-I-IM!"

(Holds up his hand. A beat. Bitterly.)

So . . . in an effort to keep the peace, and . . . satisfy the crowd, I released Barabbas to them.

(The sound of a WHIP [cue 54]. PILATE *almost cringes. Snaps his courage to finish.)*

I . . . I had Jesus severely beaten. When they had finished with Him . . . I gave the order. *(A beat. Softly.)* Crucify Him.

(He drops the scarf. Straightens. Walks out, stiffly. The whipping contin-ues. The lights fade to:

(Blackout.)

Scene Sixty-six

The Crucifixion

Officer

(Mark 15:16-32)

(The sound of a WHIP [**cue 54**]. *A camera flash goes off. Then another.*

(Lights.

(First Traveler has become the Officer. Police jacket. Hat. Baton. Marshaling a crowd back. Jaded and street tough.)

Officer: Keep movin'! Move on. Nothin' to see here.

> *(Sees us. Comes forward. Speaks to us confidentially. Flippant. As if we'll appreciate the story.)*

We had Him over there. Back of headquarters. Had the whole force out, looked like. *(A little defensive)* Just lettin' off a little steam, that's all! Little tension. We had Him dressed up in a purple robe, and some guy stuck this crown made out of thorns on His head. *(Stuffs a laugh)* Get this! Then we start salutin' Him. *(Lifts baton)* With this. "Hail!" *(Brings baton down)* BAM! "King." BAM! "Of the." BAM! "Jews!" BAM! BAM! *(Starting to realize we don't think this is funny)* Some spit on Him. Jokers were kneel-in' down, pretendin' to worship the guy! When we were through, we stuck His old clothes back on Him and dragged Him out to crucify Him.

(Getting very uncomfortable)

We stopped some yokel tourist . . . *(pulls out a note pad. Checks the name) . . .* uh, Simon Cyrene. *(Looks up)* We made him carry the Cross for His Highness. We marched Him out to Golgotha. That means "Place of the Skull." For all the right reasons. Hey, we tried to make it easy on Him! Offered Him a little drugged wine. He didn't want it. So we stretched Him out. *(A beat)* And we nailed Him up.

(Remembers the moment. The flip veneer is gone. Sees the scarf. Compul-sively wipes blood off hands.)

We started gambling to pass the time. The pot was His clothes. I'd say it was about nine o'clock when we . . . crucified Him. I noticed the sign above His head read, "The King of the Jews." Two other perps were crucified with Him. One on His right, the other over on His left. People would walk by and scream insults up at Him. "You said You'd destroy the Temple and rebuild it in three days! Come down off the Cross and save yourself!" The priests, the lawyers, and the government people were just as bad. "He 'saved' others. Let Him save His own skin!'" "Let's see the Messiah fly down off the Cross so we can see and believe!" *(Disgusted)* And the two scums crucified with Him also threw insults in His face.

(A sneer. Throws the scarf down. Stalks off.)

(Blackout)

Scene Sixty-seven

The Death of Jesus

Mary

(Mark 15:33-41)

(MUSIC [cue 55]. Sorrow theme.

(Light on MARY.

(She pulls her sweater around her. It's cold. Then she sees the scarf. Picks it up. Holds it to her.)

MARY: It was noon when the world turned black. Three hours later, He . . . cried out in a loud voice, "My God, My God, why have You forgotten Me?"

(The emotion catches her. A deep breath.)

I heard someone near me say, "Did you hear that? He's calling Elijah." Somebody ran and soaked a sponge in sour wine, stuck it on a stick, and held it up for Him to drink. "Let's see if Elijah comes to take Him down," the man next to me kept saying. Then . . . then He cried out once more. Then I heard His breath. His last. *(A beat)* That was the moment the Temple curtain was torn open. *(A long moment)* I remember the officer. *(Looks at "him")* The officer looking up at Him. I remember when he heard my Son's cry and saw how He died, he said *(resembling THE OFFICER's voice)*, "I am certain this man . . . was the Son of God."

(A beat.

(The sound of WOMEN CRYING [cue 56]. MARY looks off. Beyond tears now.)

Some of the women who had followed Him and helped His ministry were watching from a distance. Mary Magdalene, Mary the mother of James and Joses. And Salome. *(A beat)* There were many women who had come to Jerusalem with Him.

(The CRYING continues.

(**Mary** *lays the scarf on the trunk and goes out. The light fades to:*

(Blackout.)

Scene Sixty-eight

The Burial of Jesus

Pilate

(Mark 15:42-47)

(The sound of WOMEN CRYING [**cue 56**] *continues.*

(Lights. Dim.

(**Pilate** *comes in. Slowly. Painfully. Looks older and worn out. Stares at the scarf for a moment. Then turns to us.)*

Pilate: At 1800 hours, on the day before the Sabbath, Joseph of Arimathea, a respected court official—a man who had been waiting for the kingdom of God—boldly came to me and asked for the body of Jesus. *(Fights his emotion)* I was surprised to hear He had died so soon. I sent for one of the officers in charge and asked if this was the case. When I had ascertained Jesus was dead, I remanded the corpse to Joseph. *(Picks up the scarf)* I was briefed about the burial. They took a linen cloth, wrapped the body, and laid it in a tomb.

(Opens the trunk and lays the scarf inside. Gently.)

Then they rolled a stone against the entrance to it.

(Lets the lid fall. A resounding thud.)

I was told that . . . *(trying to remember)* . . . one Mary Magdalene . . . and Mary the mother of Joses saw where they laid His body.

(**Pilate** *turns and haltingly leaves. The lights hang on the trunk, then go to:*

(Blackout.)

Scene Sixty-nine

The Resurrection of Jesus
Jesus

(Mark 16:1-8)

(The stage is quiet and dark.)

(MUSIC [cue 57]. A single piano. Melodic and sparse. It begins chording. Building. More complex and full.

(Lights. Up slow. Morning colors.

(JESUS is sitting on the edge of the open trunk. Scarf around His neck. Still crumpled and lined.)

JESUS: When the Sabbath was over, Mary Magdalene, Mary the mother of James, and Salome bought spices to anoint My body. And very early in the morning on the first day of the week *(a smile)*, just as the sun was beginning to rise, they started out to visit My tomb. They had been asking each other, "Who will roll the stone away for us from the entrance to the tomb?" But when they looked up, they saw that the stone, which was quite large, had been rolled away. They ran inside and saw a young man, dressed in dazzling clothes and sitting on the right-hand side of the tomb. And they were terrified! But the man said, "Don't be afraid. You're looking for Jesus of Nazareth, who was crucified? He's not here. He's risen! Look, there's the place where His body has been. Now go and tell Peter and the other disciples that He is going on ahead of you into Galilee. There you shall see Him." But trembling with terror and dread, the women fled the tomb. And they said nothing to a soul. *(A beat)* Because they were afraid.

(JESUS stands. He takes off the scarf. Hangs it over the lid of the open trunk. He goes off. The lights fade to:

(Blackout.)

Scene Seventy

The Ends of the Earth

Three Travelers

(Mark 16:15)

(A TRAIN WHISTLE [cue 58]. *Wailing in the distance. A beat. It howls again. Coming closer. Louder. Almost deafening. It reaches its peak.*

(Lights.

(THE TRAVELERS are holding their luggage and staring up at the signpost. "JE-RUSALEM" has been taken down. The new arrow reads "THE ENDS OF THE EARTH."

(The TRAIN HOWLS and whistles past. A light wind stirs their clothes.

(The lights fade on the tableau, lingering on the open trunk. Then the lights go to:

(Blackout.)

Topical Index

Seasonal Index

Program Index

The following are some suggestions on how to collect scenes and monologues into short dramas. The arrangements are for use in holiday programs or to augment sermons, services, programs, conferences, seminars, or Bible studies.

EASTER WEEK

For a Palm Sunday or Maundy Thursday/Good Friday program or service. It requires as few as 3 actors or as many as 14.

Scene 47: The Triumphal Entry (Two Tourists)
Scene 49: The Cleansing of the Temple (Carny Man)
Scene 53: The Parable of the Vineyard (Jesus)
Scene 60: Anointing and Betrayal at Bethany (Judas)
Scene 61: The Passover Meal (Peter)
Scene 62: Gethsemane (Jesus)
Scene 63: Jesus Before the Council (Caiphas and Justices)
Scene 64: Peter's Denial (Servant Girl)
Scene 65: Jesus Before Pilate (Pilate)
Scene 66: The Crucifixion (Officer)
Scene 67: The Death of Jesus (Mary)
Scene 68: The Burial of Jesus (Pilate)
Scene 69: The Resurrection of Jesus (Jesus)

PARABLES

This collection of Jesus' parable teachings gives a vibrant portrait of Christ's storytelling power.

Scene 17: The Parable of the Seeds (Jesus)
Scene 18: Parables About the Kingdom (Jesus)
Scene 53: The Parable of the Vineyard (Jesus)

JESUS THE HEALER

This drama is a powerful look at Jesus' ministry as a healer, told from a wide spectrum of biblical characters. Scenes not arranged in Mark's chronology but for dramatic impact. Can be done with as few as 3 actors or as many as 11.

Scene 11: Healing of the Withered Hand (Levi)
Scene 5: Healing of Peter's Mother-in-law (Mother-in-Law)
Scene 7: Healing of the Leper (The Leper)
Scene 21: Healing of the Bleeding Woman and Jairus' Daughter (Jairus)
Scene 22: Jesus Rejected in Nazareth (Mary)
Scene 33: Healing of the Blind Man (Jesus)
Scene 8: Healing of the Paralytic (The Paralytic)
Scene 46: Healing of Blind Bartimaeus (Bartimaeus)
Scene 30: Healing of a Deaf Man (Jesus)

WOMEN IN THE GOSPEL

This is a drama looking at the women Jesus taught, healed, and cared for in Mark—and their work in His ministry. Can be done with as few as two actors or as many as seven.

Scene 5: Healing of Peter's Mother-in-law (Mother-in-Law)
Scene 15: Jesus' Family (Mary)
Scene 21: Healing of the Bleeding Woman and Jairus' Daughter (Jairus)
Scene 29: Healing of the Gentile Woman's Daughter (Gentile Woman)
Scene 58: The Widow's Offering (The Widow)
Scene 60: Anointing and Betrayal at Bethany (Judas)
Scene 67: The Death of Jesus (Mary)
Scene 69: The Resurrection of Jesus (Jesus)

DEMONIZATION

A look at Jesus' authority and power over demons and spirits of bondage.

Scene 4: Healing the Demoniac (Peter)
Scene 20: Healing of the Gerasene Demoniac (Rancher)
Scene 29: Healing of the Gentile Woman's Daughter (Gentile Woman)
Scene 36: Healing of a Demoniac Boy (Father)

HOLY/KINGDOM LIVING

A collection of scenes sampling Jesus' teachings on godly goals and behavior. Not arranged in Mark's chronology, but for dramatic/topical impact. Can be done with as few as three actors or as many as five.

Scene 18: Parables About the Kingdom (Jesus)
Scene 56: Jesus Questioned About Commandments (Court Reporter)
Scene 28: Jesus Dispels Empty Traditions (Jesus)
Scene 43: Jesus Talks About Treasure (Jesus)
Scene 58: The Widow's Offering (Widow)
Scene 51: Jesus Talks About Faith and Forgiveness (Jesus)
Scene 54: Jesus Questioned About Taxes (Levi)
Scene 38: Jesus Talks About Greatness (Child, Jesus)
Scene 39: Jesus Talks About Temptation (Child, Jesus)

THE KINGDOM OF GOD

A collection of scenes on the kingdom of God—parables, teachings, stories.